REDEFINING SUCCESS

God's Purpose In Building Wealth

Dawud Crayton

Extreme Overflow
PUBLISHING
Grayson, Georgia

Extreme Overflow
PUBLISHING
Grayson, Georgia

Extreme Overflow Publishing
A Brand of Extreme Overflow Enterprises, Inc
P.O. Box 1184
Grayson, GA 30017
www.extremeoverflow.com
Send feedback to info@extreme-overflow-enterprises.com

Printed in the United States of America

Editing by Yolanda Lewis Cover Design by Extreme Overflow Publishing

Library of Congress Catalogin-Publication
Data is available for this title. ISBN: 978-0-9976256-2-2

Contents

Contents (Continued)

Introduction

Entrepreneurialism is one of the keys that will open the door of opportunity for kingdom domination, purpose and an abundant financial future. God wants us to be blessed financially, emotionally and relationally. God wants us to be filled with the peace that comes from a relationship with Him. This book contains the keys that unlock the power of financial dominance; the place of blessings and purposeful position that God wants for His people, right now. With God's principles for success described in this book, anyone can apply them to their life.

Understanding your purpose in life and the authority that God gave you as His royal governing authority on this earth, gives you permission to remove any inhibition about acquiring wealth. Understanding your purpose in life and the authority that God gave you dispels the myth about there being virtue in poverty. Accepting these truths will release you to pursue abundant financial blessings and enjoy God's biblical prosperity.

There are many Christians who view wealthy people as being evil; there seems to be an association between wealth and evil. In a Christian culture many have embraced that mindset and because of this, many people will not pursue their greatest potential for building wealth. One of the biggest impediments Christians have in helping others is a lack of resources. Some Christians find that they can't help the poor because they are the poor; churches, food pantries and ministries are being closed down regularly because of a lack of funding. Many times people are only focused on their ability to make just enough money to keep their head above water. Only to later find themselves bobbing up and down financially; broke one day and just above water financially the next. God gave us the power to slam the door shut on poverty when he gave us the power to create wealth. Look at Deuteronomy 8:18 NKJV, "And you shall remember your God, for it is he who gives you the power to get wealth." In the Bible, money is mentioned over 800 times and it is not always spoken of in a negative way.

Money has always been a tool that God uses to bless his beloved people to do good work. Money is not evil; it's just a tool. Every mechanic, carpenter or tradesman knows that the more tools you have, the more options you have. The tool (or money) is not evil in the hands of the right person. A hammer in the hands of a skilled carpenter can build a house or the same hammer in the hands of an evil person can be used to bludgeon someone to death; money is the same way. Money is just a tool to carry out whatever your heart desires; if your heart is pure, good things will happen as a result and if your heart is evil, evil will result because money is just a means for conveying what is in your heart.

In this book you will find the secrets to understanding God's perspective on money and preparing your heart to receive money so that when you do get it, you will carry out good things with it. You will also find a breakdown of God's guaranteed principles for success as well as the definition of God's all encompassing success and abundant life. God doesn't just want to bless you with money but God's blessings include joy, peace, purpose, and good relationships. When you are ready to receive God's blessings, the sky is the limit. God has given you everything you need to build wealth on earth, through the scriptures. My wife and I have used these same biblical principles to move us from one of our biggest financial struggles into our greatest triumphs using God's biblical principles to propel us out of our struggle into places we never thought were possible for us.

My wife Taisha and I raised three children together; Shareese, Dawud Jr. and Isaiah. I have no doubt that God put us together and kept us together for His purpose. Today we have a better perspective on what it means to be a prosperous, purposeful and blessed family. God has kept us together through some very difficult times. There was a time when satanic attacks and financial strain tried to pull us apart. Research studies show that financial strain in a relationship is one of the leading causes of divorce (Holland, 2015). There was a time that we were so financially overwhelmed that we didn't believe we could make it as a family. Our biggest financial struggle came after September 11th when the twin towers fell and America entered into the greatest financial depression in the history of this country.

At the time, both my wife and I had six figure income jobs; my wife worked for a well known mortgage company and I worked in construction. In the months following September 11th we both lost our jobs and felt like we had no hope for taking care of our family. We were on public assistance with very little food; our house was in foreclosure and we didn't even have money to put enough gas in our car in order to go to a job interview. All we had was our faith in a God that He would never forsake us. God then gave us a vision of starting a business. Even though we had never owned a business and didn't have startup money, we believed God. Our family pulled together, prayed and gathered every penny we could find around the house. We came up with $21 dollars. With that $21 dollars we started a company that in the third year of business grossed over $2 million dollars annually. It was through this building phase that we learned many of the biblical principles in this book with regard to building wealth, creating legacy, business structure, and the true meaning of success.

Success is replicable through biblical principles. Just like a good

GPS is a guarantee for finding your destination, principles for business, life and financial success work the same way. By understanding and following the principles contained in the Bible you will undoubtedly arrive at your greatest level of success in Christ.

God created us for a purpose. God doesn't just want to bless one area of your life. He wants to bless every aspect of your life; you can win it all with Jesus! You can be blessed by God in this life and the next. The blessings of the Lord makes us rich and He adds no sorrow with it. (Proverbs 10:22) My hope is that through the principles shared in this book many families are blessed spiritually and financially with overwhelming wealth. It is the purpose of God's people to take over the earth and dominate with the wealth and influence we were created to hold by redefining success.

THE BEGINNING

". . . mature love casteth out fear: because fear hath torment . . ."

1 John 4:18

The biggest impediment for anyone's success comes from within. We all develop self doubt and impediments based on our life experiences that cause us to doubt ourselves and sabotage our own opportunities. Those negative belief systems hinder us from pursuing opportunities that God places in our pathway. These belief systems contradict the dreams we have inside that yearn for something greater but tell us we're not smart enough or good enough to achieve them. Negative belief systems come from negative experiences or events in our lives. If your parent(s) abandoned you, you may believe you're not valuable. As a result you may withdraw yourself from good relationships because you believe everyone will eventually leave you. People who are told by teachers that they'll never amount to anything can sometimes get discouraged and stop trying because they may feel worthless. When a negative experience happens to you it carries the potential to become a negative belief system. If you believe what was done to you is an indication of who your are, it becomes a belief system and a way of thinking for you. Negative belief systems can cause you to be unmotivated to strive for better. They can even cause you to sabotage good situations and opportunities in your life because you don't feel like you deserve to be happy. In order to come into success, you must identify those negative belief systems. You must acknowledge that you're better than that and reaffirm yourself. You must tell yourself that you are good enough and finally you must be willing to not settle for less than the best for yourself.

My story is one of having overcome low self-esteem; a negative belief system and mindset that would have prevented me from going after opportunities that I did not believe were attainable. In the late seventies and eighties is when I grew up and formulated many of my opinions and perceptions about myself. As a black kid during this era people of color were just beginning to be seen in positions of authority as police officers, doctors, lawyers and business owners. I developed a great deal of how I saw myself based on my environment and television programs. I saw a lot of poor black people but not too many rich ones. I saw lots of people of color on the news for crimes but not too many holding positions on the Supreme Court. Since I didn't see too many prominent people of color I began to associate my color with being a limitation for success; a negative belief system.

NEGATIVE MINDSETS DEVELOP NEGATIVE RESULTS

". . . mature love casteth out fear: because fear hath torment . . ."

1 John 4:18

I grew up in a small multicultural city called Brockton, Massachusetts. Brockton was known as a very tough city. The renowned boxer, Marvin Hagler, came out of Brockton. Brockton was a culturally diverse city and for the most part people in Brockton got along pretty well. However, we were still coming out of a lot of the racial discrimination prevalent in previous eras. Black and white children would hang around with each other but not too much to avoid being labeled as disloyal to their own race.

My father moved us to Brockton when we were babies. We lived in a little three bedroom ranch house in a nice, quiet neighborhood. My father was a very hard working man; he was a school teacher and he also had several jobs in addition to going to school at night. For the most part, my mother was a stay at home mom. Our parents had four children; Huston, me and the twins: Stefan, and Adia. Stefan and Adia were four years younger than my brother and I. My older brother Huston was less than a year older than me so my parents kind of had two sets of twins; my brother and I were twins for a month every year. The special thing about us was that we were inseparable. As kids, we slept in the same bed and shared everything. If you saw one of us, the other wasn't far away. We fought all the time but we loved each other no less. We were fierce protectors of each other, which was good because we grew up in a city where you had to know how to fight if you didn't want to get bullied.

In our elementary years, Brockton was a multicultural city but our neighborhood and schools were predominantly white. We were the only black boys our age in our neighborhood. At elementary age we would walk down to the neighborhood park where all the kids would congregate and play. If there was a neighborhood game like kick the can, red light green light, or freeze tag, that is where it took place. If there was going to be a fight after school that was where it would take place. There were miles of woods surrounding the neighborhood park where we would run through with the neighborhood kids and play all sorts of games. We would whittle sticks into toy guns and play Army, cops and robbers, and every other game that our imagination would take us to.

We learned early on from our white friends that we would make the best robbers. We agreed to play the robber even though we didn't like it. We cooperated because they felt that we fit the profile better than our white friends. We saw tons of black bad guys on TV but we didn't remember seeing any black cops so that role was off limits to us when there was a white kid that could fit the role perfectly. The truth is I wanted to be the good guy, I wanted my hair to be blonde, long and to flap in the wind but when I looked in the mirror, I only saw the bad guy.

". . . mature love casteth out fear: because fear hath torment . . ."

1 John 4:18

As young children around the ages of 7 to 9 we were totally oblivious to racial hatred and bigotry. Over time we began to notice that we weren't treated the same as all the other children. Some of the neighborhood adults would treat the white kids with respect but treated us as though they expected us to be bad.

My brother and I began to develop unhealthy comparisons of ourselves with others. We began to see ourselves as less valuable in our own eyes. I developed a negative perception of myself and took on feelings of inadequacy. This was the onset of my view and perception of myself being molded by racial stereotypes, situations, statements and stigmas that were unloaded on me by some of the kids in school and from my neighborhood. We weren't told we could be the president of the United States, instead we heard that there would never be a black president in America and if there was, he'd be dead before his first term was over. We didn't see a lot of successful black business owners in real life or on television. As far as we knew, black people were limited to certain occupations; crime being the most common.

There were two young men growing up who had a particularly profound effect on shaping our view of people of color and how we saw ourselves (as people of color). To protect their identity, we'll refer to them as Dick and John. They introduced us to a level of racial brainwashing, intimidation, abuse and hatred which affected how we saw ourselves. This experience with Dick and John played a huge role in affecting my lack of confidence and pursuing opportunities. I believed what they said about me and because of that I lived with a sense of hopelessness. I didn't believe I had the right pedigree to be smart enough to pursue the same opportunities as white people and be successful. Dick and John did most of their evil work on us at our neighborhood park.

Dick and John were much older teenage boys who used to be at the park and they would always talk to me and my brother Huston every chance they got. They knew we were innocent and totally ignorant to their hatred towards people of color. They saw us as an opportunity to get away with expressing all the evil and hatred they had for people of color without receiving any consequences. They made it their life mission to find and bully us whenever they saw us. At the very least, they would always make remarks about the inferiority of black people and use racial slurs like "nigger," "coon," and "shine." They exposed us to black pornography magazines and gave us a very perverse and twisted crash course on the birds and the bees. They would be nice enough to us to keep us from running away but before we'd leave they would always leave us with a shot in the jaw or a kick in the nuts. "Awe! Don't cry. That didn't hurt you. Niggers can take a lot of pain," they'd say. I know we believed it because we were later known for punching ourselves in the nose until blood gushed out telling people, "It don't hurt me! I'm a real nigga! I can take a lot of pain!" They would make us say these words about ourselves and our parents. They would say, "Call yourself a nigger!" We would respond, "I'm a nigger!" And they would laugh. We didn't know what the words meant; we were young and totally ignorant to racial hatred. We would laugh with them in hopes that they would be nicer to us. We were young and we wanted these cool older teenage kids to be our friends.

We would try to do things to make them like us or at least not beat us up as much. Dick would pretend he was being nice and say, "Hey buddy! Let me push you on the swing." We would get on and he would push us as high as he could on the swing and when the swing wouldn't go any higher he would knock us off and send us flying through the air to come crashing down to the ground. He'd always finish up with a mean comment like, "It's hard to break a nigger's neck." They were relentless in their efforts to dehumanize and emasculate us. After so many months of their hazing we smartened up and were much more careful in trying to avoid them but they would make sure they came and found us wherever we were. They were getting more and more brazen with their attacks. We grew to be terrified of Dick and John and the worst part about it was they told us if we told anyone they would kill us. We were too afraid to tell so we had to suffer their torment in silence.

". . . mature love casteth out fear: because fear hath torment . . ."

1 John 4:18

I remember the time they held me at the park and told my brother they would kill me if he didn't steal money from my father's wallet and give it to them. My brother stole the money, gave it to them and when my father found out Huston stole the money, he got a spanking from my father. We preferred a spanking from my dad rather than to face the wrath of Dick and John. I also remember the time they took our brand new bow and arrow set and shot the arrows so far into the woods we couldn't find it and we got in trouble for losing the bow and arrow the first day we got it. There were many more attacks from them. Like the time they took us out on an ice pond and smashed my brother's head on the ice to see if a "niggers" head was hard enough to crack the ice. I remember it like it was yesterday.

It was beginning to become normal for us to take a beating from Dick and John. Over time they persisted in saying things like, "Niggers should die!" or "The only jobs you'll be able to have are butlers shining my shoes, niggers." Or "You Niggas won't ever be rocket scientist."

They would always tell us about how niggers were a dirty mark on our society and we believed them. A lot of the things they said about black people being criminals, seemed to be true based on what we saw on the news and on television shows. In our young minds their comments proved to be true; black people would very commonly be the bad guys.

We attributed our mistreatment with the color of our skin. Overtime I wanted hair like them and wondered why my skin was so dark.

It always made me stand out in my predominantly white neighborhood. I just wanted to fit in with everyone else. I wanted to be like the cool guys on TV; Bow and Luke, Duke from the Dukes of Hazard, and Starsky and Hutch who were my favorite cops on TV; those white guys were cool. I didn't want to be the bad black guys. I wanted my hair to flow in the wind when we got in a cool convertible. I wanted to be a successful business owner like the white people. I didn't want to be the bad guy with the nappy hair and the ugly dark skin. I didn't want to be what the older teenagers called me and I began to see myself as not being as good as the white kids that looked down on me.

The truth of the matter was not that I didn't like the color of my skin; I just didn't like being mistreated because of the color of my skin. I actually liked being black but I hated how I was viewed by some people for being black. I had developed a negative perception of what it meant to be black. There was nothing wrong with the color of my skin; it was the portrayal of the color that messed me up. My little afro was good hair; the water would bead up on it, and my skin never burned from the sun. But my negative association with my skin complexion completely affected how I perceived myself. It wasn't until I learned the pride of my African American culture that I realized that the problem wasn't the color of my skin, it was how the people with the color of my skin were treated and portrayed. The culture we lived in and the people around us made us feel like our color was bad and excluded from success.

We finally got to the point where we had to tell our parents about what had been going on at the park. Dick and John had gone too far when they devised a plan to abduct, torture, and kill us. On this day my brother and I were the only boys at the park. There were acres of woods surrounding the park. The wooded area surrounding the park was big enough to where no one would be able to hear our screams. This was the day that Dick and John decided to execute their plan to kill us.

That day, the two older boys lured us deep into the woods with a cute kitten they had stolen from someone in the neighborhood. Once we were deep enough in the woods they smashed the kitten's head on a rock and then dragged and beat us to the designated area they had set up for us. They did horrendous things to us and at some point during their torture my brother Huston broke free and ran away. They used the same tactic as they had done in the past, they used me for ransom. They told him if he didn't come back they were going to kill me. Huston returned and got the worst of the torture for the remainder of our time with them. After they finished sticking things in us, humiliating us, making us eat things, and beating us, they made us lay our heads on a big log.

The boys grabbed two large boulders to smash our heads with. They raised the boulders up above our heads ready to send them crashing down on our skulls when John exclaimed, "Wait! If they find out we killed them we'll never get out of jail!" They argued about killing us but in the end John convinced Dick not to kill us that day. After arguing and convincing Dick not to go through with it, they let us go with their usual threat, "I'll kill you if you tell anyone." We hobbled home as fast as we could and we were too scared to tell but this time we were late coming home. We couldn't sneak upstairs and cleanup before our parents could see us this time because we were late. We couldn't lie our way out of this one because daddy was home with belt in hand waiting for an explanation as to why we were late. Our clothes were ripped, and we were covered in mud and there was too much blood not to tell them something. We were still terrified of Dick and John and even more ashamed of what they did to us to tell our parents the truth about what happened. Girls tell everything but little boys will keep a secret forever. We just couldn't bring ourselves to tell them everything; we were ashamed. So as they questioned and prodded us for answers, all they got out of us was that they beat us up, called us niggers and made us eat bugs and leaves.

I had never seen my father so upset. Daddy went over to Dick's house and confronted Dick and the old man who was his guardian. Daddy called the police and pressed charges against the two boys. We were still too scared to tell all that they had done to us or to testify in court against them. Because of that, the crime was never prosecuted as it should have been. The boys got off with a slap on the wrist and a restraining order. We were grateful for John saving our lives in the woods that day but I still remember not thinking much about the value of my life. We were innocent kids and we didn't believe anyone would hurt a kid, but for some reason we didn't feel like our lives were very valuable. We definitely didn't feel like we were as valuable as white kids. We spent the years following engaged in risky behaviors because if we died, we felt it was no great loss.

My brother became known as, "Huey Credit" or "Super Credit" because he would never turn down a dare and all of the kids had to give him credit for being the craziest. It didn't matter what the dare was or if it was guaranteed to end his life, he would do it because we no longer valued our lives. His reckless behavior included jumping from building rooftops to building rooftops, playing Russian roulette, running in front of speeding cars, running from police officers; the list was endless. Whatever it was, Huston would do it. I was afraid every day we went out that someone would dare him to do something that would end his life. He had almost died when he jumped his BMX bike off a rooftop and landed on his face. I wasn't there with him that time and the kids that dared him ran away when they saw him land on his face because they thought he was dead. My poor crazy brother laid there bleeding on the ground for hours unconscious until a man from a power company saw him laying there and called 911. When we got to the hospital I didn't even recognize my brother because his face was so disfigured. He spent weeks in the hospital and even that didn't stop him from his risky behaviors.

I engaged in risky behaviors also and I believed I was a bad kid. I hated myself for being bad. I would overeat because food gave me comfort and was an escape for me. I would get into trouble running the streets with my brother starting fights, breaking into buildings and doing anything that was mischievous or exciting because I didn't think much of myself. When I would be by myself I would stick needles in my body, punch myself in the nose until blood came out or cut myself because I hated myself and thought I deserved to die. I believed I was a bad seed who did bad things. My parents wondered why we used to get so many bloody noses because our noses used to bleed randomly. We had developed a belief system about us; we were no good. When you have a negative experience with someone or something happens to you, it carries the potential to become a belief system. When my math teacher called me, "a waste of a life," I had the option of dismissing it and saying, "No I'm not, I will get better in my behavior and I'll learn math," but I didn't. I believed him. I believed I was a waste of a life and I became what I believed just as the bible says in Proverbs 23:7, "as a man thinketh in his heart, so is he."

I was ashamed of the things that happened to me. For many years I was ashamed of the things I did. I allowed them to define me and dictate who I was and how I should behave. If a man believes he is a dog, he'll crawl around and bark like a dog. You will become what you think you are. Huston and I thought we were criminals and a waste of a life so we engaged in risky and criminal behavior. We were told good things by our parents but we chose to believe the negative things that had been said to us and we became what we believed.

In the days following the incident with Dick and John we began to tell my father about some of the conversations leading up to the last assault. We learned about the history behind some of the words like, "nigger, coon, and shine." In sharing with our father he saw that there were warning signs we should have been able to pick up on so he began to educate us on what racism meant. We watched every episode of Roots, we learned about slavery and the history of racism in this country and he began to instill in us a sense of pride for our heritage.

We would say, "I'm black and I'm proud," but the seed of low self-worth had already been planted at this point. It would take many years to really develop a true understanding of my worth. The treatment we received by the two older teenagers would be followed up for many years by school teachers, store clerks, coaches, random people and police officers who felt like they could just randomly give us a beating and send us on our way whenever they felt like searching us. It was going to take time to heal and God's power to overcome racial stereotypes in the media, and from verbal and physical attacks that would continue to be carried out by a minority of racist individuals who thought they were better than us by virtue of their skin color.

A true understanding of my value wouldn't come until years later through understanding and studying the word of God. It was difficult to kill the seed of the negative belief system that had already taken root and my brother and I didn't value our lives anymore. If someone could just kill us like dogs then we can't be very valuable, we thought. We didn't see many people who looked like us and were successful so when we behaved in accordance with our negative belief system it was reflected in our school grades and in our behavior. Many of the people we hung out with were criminals and people like us who didn't see the value in their lives. Nor did they see a hope for a brighter future. We got into trouble every chance we could because we believed that trouble was all that life held for us. There was a sense of hopelessness for our future, we didn't believe we could be business owners or successful in life in-spite of the encouragement we received from our parents.

SEEING THINGS DIFFERENTLY

"...the devil you know is better than the devil you don't know.
I finally got to the point where I refused to live with devils!"

The summer of my junior year in high school my father was coming home from work and as he passed all the prostitutes, drug dealers and criminals on Main Street he recognized two teenage boys mingled amongst all of the sordid individuals; he saw his sons! He pulled over, told us to get in the car, and at that moment, he decided we were moving out of Brockton. My father grew up in one of the toughest neighborhoods in Roxbury, Massachusetts so he immediately discerned what we were doing out there. Daddy had street smarts and he knew we were up to no good. Hanging on those corners was going to land us in one of two places; jail or the graveyard. Daddy tried his best to get us to do better in school and stay out of trouble but with no results. It was time to change our environment and we did. Daddy built a house in the nearby town of Easton, Massachusetts. He enrolled me in Oliver Ames High School which was an almost exclusively white upper class school. Oliver Ames High School had an estimated 98% college turnout rate.

Oliver Ames was a lot different than Brockton high which had over 5 thousand students and was so overcrowded you could literally sit in the back of the class, never open a book and most teachers wouldn't notice. There were so many students there. The teachers were overwhelmed with kids. Brockton High had many fights, much crime, drugs, and even in-school prostitution. If you weren't a very strong and driven student you would have a hard time taking advantage of the educational resources there. So before we knew it daddy sent my brother Huston to the Army and I went to Oliver Ames to finish my last year of high school.

I went to my new high school with a major chip on my shoulder. I was pissed that I had to leave all my friends in Brockton to go to an all white school where I doubted I would be accepted. By this time in my life I had suffered enough discrimination that I had become skeptical and suspicious going to a school that was primarily white. My neighborhood was also predominantly white and that didn't always work out well for me. I was a little suspicious of white people; I was ready to be discriminated against and I couldn't wait because I was just itching to give a "tune up" to some racist white kids. I went to school ready to fight but I didn't get what I was looking for. I had all my most violent friends on speed dial ready to pile in cars to head to Easton for a riot but I never even got an excuse. What I did learn being there was the culture was much different than any other school I had attended before. The classes were much smaller, and the teachers paid more attention to the students. I couldn't cut class anymore because the teachers noticed me. There was nothing to do in school but school work; no more fighting, cutting class, skipping school, and taking naps in the back of the class. Everyone was focused on doing their work, and not only just doing it, they did it with excellence because they had an agenda which was success.

I finally got to the point where I refused to live with devils!

Where I came from, the kids that got in the most trouble were the cool kids; over here, the smart kids got the most attention. Everyone did their homework, so when I came in without my homework assignment complete, I looked like a fool; so I made sure my homework was completed every day. These kids driven for success, there was no sense of hopelessness like in the neighborhoods I hung in. These kids were confident of the brightness of their future.

The teachers would ask questions about who sees themselves in the future owning a business or becoming a CEO of the company and everyone's hand would go up except mine. If this question was asked in Brockton there would have been a lot less hands going up. A lot of the kids in my other high school classes were planning on making a career of selling drugs. The kids in Easton had parents who were business owners and CEOs of companies; they had high-paying jobs and had inherited money from relatives. These kids were surrounded by success and filled with bright futures. Most of the kids in Easton had two parent homes and it was instilled in them that they were good enough to become whatever they desired. They weren't told that starting a business is too risky to go after. These kids were being mentored on how to start a business because their parents or family friends owned businesses. They were being encouraged and trained to take calculated risks, assessing the market, counting the cost and proceeding with caution. They were learning business principles at an early age from experts in the field.

There seemed to be no self-esteem issues associated with their ability to excel in life. I also noticed some things about how these kids carried themselves. They didn't have to have the fanciest clothes or spend an excessive amount of energy on their appearance. In other words if you accidentally stepped on someone's shoes you wouldn't get shot. When I attended Brockton High, I had to wear brand-new sneakers and designer clothes because if I didn't, I felt like a bum. But with these kids, clothes didn't seem to affect how they felt about themselves at all. Their self esteem didn't seem to be determined by external influences. It seemed to have come from within. I needed nice clothes and I needed to compare myself to others because my esteem came from external influences but when you removed those things I had nothing to feel good about.

I didn't have inner confidence and because of that I passed up many opportunities in my life. My self-esteem and my perception of myself affected the decisions I made in life. I wouldn't go after certain jobs because I didn't think I could get them. I wouldn't pick certain majors in school because I didn't think I could pass the courses. And even if I did pass the courses I didn't think I could get a job working in certain areas. The way I viewed myself prevented me from being who I wanted to be and doing what I wanted to do. All of my internal issues shaped my life and it wasn't until I put those issues aside that I would be able to pursue my dreams.

The success mentality that the white kids at Oliver Ames had began to rub off on me. Initially I didn't think I could pass my classes because I thought all these white kids were smarter than me. I thought I was just going to be the token dumb black kid, but I found that I was just as smart as most of the other kids. They weren't all geniuses; they just gave a descent effort and did their work. I wrote a paper in English class and the teacher thought it was so good she shared it with the class. I began to see myself differently. I began to form friendships with some of the kids in the classes and develop confidence in my ability to do my work. I started thinking about going to college and making a good life for myself.

I finally got to the point where I refused to live with devils!

In time I began to see things differently. I began to believe in myself and even if I never saw anyone like me succeed at something that had never been done before, I would be the first.

As time went on my confidence in myself grew, I got into junior college and began to see promise for my life. I was passing my courses and working two jobs.

One of the summer jobs I had was an enlightening turning point for me. I worked for a small painting company that was owned by a pretty successful black business owner. Mr. Walker was his name and there was nothing supernatural or spectacular about him. He wasn't a genius and he didn't levitate across the earth the way I thought business owners did. He was a normal guy that did the best he could and apparently it paid off for him. Mr. Walker had a pretty successful business with about 15 employees and enough consistent work to keep them all very busy. This was where I started to see myself in business one day. For so long owning a business was so off limits to me that I hadn't entertained the idea of owning my own business.

Growing up I was always taught to look for a safe reliable job. I remember looking up to people who were entrepreneurs but never believed it was something I was capable of pulling off. I was taught that opening a business was a very risky thing to do. I believed you needed millions of dollar and master's degrees in business in order to run a successful business. Most businesses failed in the first year and 8 out of 10 businesses don't last more than a few years. This was a risk we were taught that you should never take. You should always take the safe route. I remember the saying, "the devil you know is better than the devil you don't know." I finally got to the point where I refused to live with devils! I can be anything God has called me to be and do all things through Christ who strengthens me.

It was that summer that I began to believe that I would one day own my own business. I was beginning to dream about one day owning my own business. I began to see myself differently. Maybe I was smarter and more eligible for success than I thought I was.

How we see ourselves determines our position because if you can't see yourself in the position then you may sabotage or walk away from the opportunity. You are a child of the most high God. He called you his child which makes you heirs to everything that your father owns; if it's on this earth it's not off limits to you.

LITTLE IN YOUR OWN EYES

And Samuel said, "Though you are little in your own eyes, are you not the head of the tribes of Israel? The Lord anointed you king over Israel. And Samuel told him, "Although you may think little of yourself, are you not the leader of the tribes of Israel? The Lord has anointed you king of Israel.

Samuel 15:17

What do you think of yourself? People or cultural influences may have told you negative things about you that are not true. But if you believe them, you will hold yourself in low regard. If you think negatively about yourself, you become "little in your own eyes," and it will affect your confidence and ability to do great things. Great people do great things. You've got to see yourself as great before you can expect to pursue greatness.

Your life experiences and how you see yourself will affect your destiny. If you see yourself as little, you will do little things. But if you see how big God sees you, you can accomplish the big things that He has in store for you.

Saul was not little, but he saw himself as little. How he saw himself had nothing to do with his looks or stature because the bible says he was a head taller and more handsome than any other man in Israel. What he lacked was confidence. He didn't believe in himself and because of that he made hasty decisions. Even though he received victory after victory he never had the confidence and faith that he could do it again. It was almost as if he felt like he got lucky in winning rather than being gifted and chosen by God to do His good work. It was as though he expected failure and was surprised by success. Confident people expect success. He didn't see himself as gifted. He didn't see himself as chosen and capable enough to pull off great things. I imagine that he might have felt like he was scamming his way through the position of kingship. His lack of confidence showed that he didn't feel qualified for the position. If you don't feel qualified for a position you will be afraid of being exposed as unqualified. You may even feel intimidated by anyone that is gifted because in your mind their gift is a comparison tool for pointing out your incompetency. Valuing yourself and your position is the best way to tear down feelings of jealousy and intimidation. When you know your value and value your position you're not worried about someone taking your position because nobody can beat you at being you.

Saul's jealousy raged within him when the people complimented David's fighting ability. A confident leader would have taken that as a compliment on his leadership ability. Saul wasn't a soldier, he was the leader; leaders don't fight, they lead. Recognizing that there is a designated position for you, seeing yourself great and being confident in your position are essential components of success. Nobody can better perform a job that God designed for you than you. Saul was suspicious and insecure because he didn't see the value in himself. When God puts you in a position you don't have to be insecure in, how to keep your job. What God has for you is for you only and nobody can take your place.

People who see themselves as little want the focus on them because it makes them feel better about themselves. They need constant validation from everyone around them because they don't feel good about themselves. They gravitate toward external things to boost their self worth because they don't see the worth that is in them. It's unhealthy comparing yourself to others because you can never be somebody else. You must learn to love who you are. You must know that nobody can be a better you than you and you must embrace the greatness inside you. You cannot compare yourself to other people or try to do what other people do. You must be secure in knowing who you are and be comfortable living in your own skin.

Our life experiences help to shape who we are, how we perceive ourselves and the opportunities in front of us. Allowing negative experiences and things people say about you to permeate the fabric of your being and influence how you see yourself, can prevent you from taking advantage of the good opportunities in life that are in front of you. Life and opportunity are all about your perception and if you go at life with a positive view of yourself and a positive perception of yourself you will be successful.

We miss opportunities because our eyes are not open to the reality that we can achieve the highest levels of success. Until the election of President Obama many people never believed that they could be president of the United States. Many people never believed that they could be business owners, doctors, lawyers, neurosurgeons and millionaires. People that grew up in broken homes or experienced broken marriages sometimes don't believe that they can have a successful marriage or that they can find a husband that will love them and stay with them. People stop believing based on their experience; their environment has hindered them from taking advantage of opportunities that they don't believe they are qualified for.

Negative life experiences and negative self perception affects people generationally. One generation can only pass on to the next generation what they know, and if the best that they know is simply surviving then the following generation will have a difficult time trying to figure out how to go beyond what they have been taught.

How we see ourselves determines our position because if you can't see yourself in the position then you may sabotage or walk away from the opportunity. You are a child of the most high God. He called you His child and that makes you heir to everything that your father owns; nothing is off limits to you.

Overcoming low self-esteem issues and your perception of who you are and your abilities are important because they will affect how you approach your opportunities. If you allow inner issues to prevent you from accepting or going after opportunities you will miss the greatest you. You will forfeit your greatest successes. Your perception of your situation is the difference between losing and gaining. If you perceive something as an opportunity or perceive that you were able to access it as an opportunity then it will become an opportunity.

PAIN.
PURPOSE.
PROSPERITY.

"My Father! If it is possible, let this cup of suffering be taken away from me"

Matthew 26:39

God allows us to go through some very painful experiences in life. There are many situations in life that we must endure but they are the only ways to develop us and give us the keys to our success. A preacher once told me that the only way to achieve success is by going through every step that other successful people before you have taken. There is no magical way to jump into passion, promise and prosperity; you must fight, train and work your way into your destiny. Jesus had to suffer and die on the cross against his wishes, "My Father! If it is possible, let this cup of suffering be taken away from me" (Matthew 26:39). He did it because it was the only way to save our souls. The only way to success is to live out the sometimes painful principles that lead to success.

Webster's dictionary defines 'Theodicy,' as a defense of God's goodness and omnipotence in view of the existence of evil. In other words it's a theological term that is used by God's people to explain why a good God allows such evil to continue in this world. My short answer is God will not remove the gift of free will from the earth and he uses the negative experiences to work together for our greater good. And we know that all things work together for good to those who love God, to those who are the called according to His purpose (Romans 8:28).

Life is full of vicissitudes but our free will gives us the right to build up or to destroy this earth. We have the free will to infringe on the rights of others or to bring justice, because when God gives a gift he will not retract it. "For God's gifts and his call can never be withdrawn." (Romans 11:29)

God is all knowing and because of that he uses the negative experiences in life as developmental tools. God uses our negative life experiences to draw greatness and resolve out of us. Just as you'll never get juice out of an orange without squeezing it, you will never know the greatness within if you never suffer through the pressures and pain of life.. God teaches us through our pain.

John Maxwell once said, "Pain produces passion and passion will lead you to your purpose." Passion cannot be taught or bought. Passion is something that you must suffer for; it is a yearning and a burning on the inside of you that is awakened by an injustice or an area of need. Many times it can be said that the greater the injustice the greater the passion. Martin Luther King had passion brought on by his pain. Where would we as a country be if he had not suffered injustices? Would he have the drive to give his life for the cause of freedom, unity and equality? Would he have the passion to endure death threats against him and his family? Some people are ok with being oppressed until they realize their oppressors are just going to kill them anyway and it is only then that they develop enough passion to fight back. It's only through the heat of that passion that gives them the strength to overpower the opposition and become victorious.

It's at the low points in life where you have been in dangerous places, dangerous situations, discouraged, experience loss of family members, loss of relationships, loss of jobs, sickness, depression, that will cause you to hit rock bottom but this is where your strength and passion is developed. The valleys and the low places in life that could have killed you; God spares your life. With God's grace those valley experiences prove to serve as development of the strength, wisdom, insights, resolve to fight, passion and determination to fight your way to the prize.

Always remember that your low points in life are an indication that you are one step closer to walking out your calling and purpose in life.

I remember operating a crane on a barge in the Boston Harbor; in Massachusetts. A construction demolition company had previously blown up an old dilapidated bridge that previously connected Long Island to Moon Island in Quincy, Massachusetts. I was working for a company on a barge with a diving team to reclaim the granite stones from the bottom of the ocean for the purposes of rebuilding the footings that previously supported the bridge. I would lower the cable from my crane

Figure 1- *Granite Stone*

deep into the water and the underwater divers began to rig the stones for me to pull them up on the deck of the barge. We had extracted a few stones when I realized that there was a large granite stone that came up but was broken in half. I thought that was peculiar because the other stones were completely intact. A half hour later I pulled up the other half of the broken stone and lowered it onto the deck next to the other broken stone.

I sat and watched the stone mason go over and fashion the stones together with an epoxy. I asked the stone mason, "Why didn't you just throw that stone away and get another one?" He responded, "Are you crazy! I would never throw away a stone like this! There are no two just alike in the world. These stones are too valuable to just throw away." He continued, "This is the cornerstone and it is stronger than all the other stones. It serves a unique purpose of being the foundational support for the bridge and when I'm finished with it, it will be even stronger than the stones that were never broken." The stone mason went on to explain to me that the epoxy he used is one of the strongest adhesives in the world and if you were to try to pull the stones apart it would break everywhere but where it had already been broken.

We are like that stone that was reclaimed. We are uniquely designed for a purpose and even though we may have been broken, we serve a purpose that is so unique; we are the only ones on earth that can do it.

You may have thought you were trash; people in your life may have thrown you away. As the stone mason of our lives; God understands just how valuable we are. God knows how to rebuild us as if we were never broken. Even when a bone is broken and healed it forms a callous at the site of the break where calcium is deposited so that the bone is strongest at the place of the break. The areas we are broken in, after they heal become the strongest. Some were broken by drug addiction and when we are healed we become the greatest drug counselors with insight that touches the lives of former addicts in ways that the greatest psychologist and most educated drug rehab therapist in the world will never be able to. You can't receive that kind of power by chance, you must suffer for it. There is no better way to have insight than to be broken and even though we didn't want it or ask for it, we are stronger because of it.

Just like a vaccine contains some of the pathogens that make you sick, your places of hurt are the vaccine for strengthening you in life. But those situations weren't allowed to kill us. What didn't kill you, made you strong enough to fight off future attacks. With the antibody of God's grace, His strength is in your blood. You are better and stronger than you have ever been. Can't you feel it?

You are the walking living antidote for others who have suffered like you. You came through your trial, survived it and you are the answer to winning that fight. You are made more than a conqueror (Romans 8:37).

The adversity in our lives gives us a passion to help others in the areas we were hurt in. We can empathize and reach those who are suffering like we once suffered. If you are looking for your calling and purpose in life, start looking in the areas you were broken in.

SEEING THE OPPORTUNITY WHEN YOU'RE LOSING

"For the Lord God is a sun and shield; the Lord will give grace and glory; no good thing will He withhold from those who walk uprightly."

Psalms 84:11

In my career as an operating engineer I have suffered many setbacks and obstacles that were so devastating, I've felt like digging up a grave to jump in. Otherwise I was going have to start my own business in order to take care of my family. The latter proved to be the best solution.

The onset of my career began with a four year apprenticeship to become an operating engineer. During the time of the apprenticeship I would go to classes two nights a week with eight-hour trainings every other Saturday. Upon completion I was appointed to a job as an operator and made great money. There I learned how to operate and repair various types of heavy construction equipment. The apprenticeship gave me experience repairing and operating everything from tower cranes hung 300 feet in the air to underground tunnel boring machines, experimental equipment, bull dozers, excavators, Gradall excavators and more. If it's used in construction I have probably operated and repaired it before.

" . . . no good thing will He withhold from those who walk uprightly."

Psalms 84:11

Prior to September 11th 2001, the construction industry in Massachusetts was booming. In the years following, construction work slowed down tremendously. I had finished my apprenticeship and was working as a full journeyman operator; I had a very difficult time staying employed. There were tons of operators from the Big Dig with only a handful of jobs available. I would work about 5 to 8 months a year; I would get called by my Job Placement agent to start a job during the months of March and April. Once the construction season was coming to a close, around October or November I would be the first person to get laid off without any hope of returning to work until the next year around March or April. During the season if I worked for any contractor they could lay me off at any time for any reason.

I remember a time when I was outside on a rainy day fixing a broken machine in the mud and I went next to an office trailer to grab a tool out of a tool box that was right next to an open window. A new operator was in the trailer with the bosses instead of working like I was. I overheard him express his concern for being laid off because they weren't going to need his machine anymore. As I stood there, he complained about affirmative action and how black people have it so easy and the boss interrupted him and said, "Don't worry, we have our own affirmative action policy here, we're laying off the nigger!" I was the only "nigger" on the job so I knew my days were numbered just like every other job. There was nothing I could do to fight against the discrimination. I was laid off soon after that conversation with no hope of suing them or going back to work. If I tried to sue them I would lose the lawsuit because I had no proof, and the union would label me as a trouble maker. When I called my agent for a job they would suddenly have a shortage of opportunities for me. Once you get the reputation of being a trouble maker nobody wants you. There were very few people of color in my line of business so there was nobody to go to for help.

I did my best on every job I went to. I would be at work an hour early every day. I made sure I tried to work harder than everyone on the job in hopes that they would keep me. There was nothing more that I could do to try and keep my job. I knew this wasn't the only time I had been laid off because of the color of my skin and I knew in this business it wouldn't be the last. I know that not every company I work for was like that but there were enough of them that I wasn't comfortable with putting the security of my family and finances in the hands of people who don't care about me. I remember saying to myself, "God, you blessed me with a great family, how am I supposed to take care of them?" At that moment I decided there is nothing more I can do in trying to keep my job so we were going to have to start a business. Over the course of the next few years I was paying attention to more than just my job. I was connecting with good people who had great connections in the business world. I met some of the owners of the companies I worked for as well as key people in high positions. I heard about subcontractor opportunities and I began to pray for God to give me just one chance.

I finally got that chance years later. It wasn't in the area I wanted to be in, which was in heavy equipment, but it was my foot in the door for being in business. My opportunity came after my wife and I were both laid off. My union made money available from my retirement for a loan. I took as much money as I could and we decided we would start two businesses. My wife would do taxes and I would support her while seeking opportunities to get my first job doing land clearing or construction work.

We found the cheapest little office building space in a basement of a pizza shop that was right near a busy area with lots of people who were available for tax season which was about a month and a half away in January. We even had to split the rent with a friend. By January we had almost completely run out of money but we were still hopeful because we were all set for Taisha to do taxes.

". . . no good thing will He withhold from those who walk uprightly."

Psalms 84:11

At any minute we were expecting hundreds of people to walk through those doors with cash in hand and we were going to have a prosperous business and pay off all our debts with millions. A few days went by and nobody came in. One day I went outside and I noticed right across the street from us was a beautiful expensive building with the visibility of the entire city; it was a national tax service company. We wanted to rent out an office space there but couldn't afford it. I was pretty much done at that point. There was no way we were going to be able to compete with these guys. The only taxes we were going to get were referrals. They took any chance of walk-ins out the picture which left us with virtually no business at all. By this time we were dead broke. There was no chance at all that I could get a job during the cold months of the year so I asked my wife, what do you do when you don't even get an opportunity. Her response was, "You create an opportunity."

It's a blessing to have such an optimistic wife and partner because how you perceive your losses is the determining factor for your outcome. We put our heads together and began to think of what else we could do. It was a great time for us to pursue a construction project or something I could do to make money. We bumped our fists and at that moment we were going to turn this loss into millions.

With every loss there is always opportunity, you just have to see the opportunity in the loss. Taisha called her connections in the real estate business. Taisha was very well known to Realtors after working in the mortgage industry for so many years and it just so happened that there was a real estate office above us that was in dire need of contractors to service foreclosures. After September 11th the economy went right down the toilet and as a result there were millions of houses that went in foreclosure all at the same time. Up until this point in time contractors that worked on foreclosures were unheard of because this amount of work for this industry didn't exist; or wasn't worth the time.

With this opportunity, we had an exclusive leg up into an industry that most contractors had never even heard of. We had virtually no competition at all. We had the opportunity to build a business that was exceedingly, abundantly and above all we could ask or think. I didn't need a million dollar loan to buy equipment, bonding or any of the things I thought I needed to startup our business. Besides, by this time we only had a couple hundred dollars left in the bank. With the money we had left we bought the necessary insurances. Taisha did the business name logo and made sure all of the business prerequisites were taken care of. Finally, we were ready; shortly after picking up our first contract.

We got our first work order and I was terrified of the unknown. I decided that I wasn't going to let fear get the best of me; I was going to have to do it afraid. I wasn't sure of what would be expected of me but I knew the same God that presented the opportunity would make provision for me to carry it out. I was so excited and scared. It was about 3:30 in the afternoon smack dab in the middle of a MA winter. In MA it starts getting dark around 4:00 pm in the winter time. I was so anxious and worried about finishing the job within the allowable time frame that against my wife's advisement I decided I was going to start this new job that night.

There was just one problem. The job was about an hour away; in Cape Cod, and we were broke. We were so broke I wanted to open a Gmail account, just so we could eat the spam. We couldn't beg for or borrow another dollar so we went through the house and found every penny we we could find. The kids gave us all their pennies and I had the idea to cash them in for dollars at the Coinstar Machine at Walmart. My wife said Coinstar takes about seven cent on every dollar and we needed every red cent. We took those pennies down to the local bank and put them into rolls. We cashed them in and what we had was $21 dollars and a little change left over. I had enough money to drive to my first job.

With that $21 dollars we did our first job and with the money we got from that first job we continued to grow. If I had never been laid off, we would have never started our business. If I hadn't suffered so many years being laid off, talked about, yelled at and mistreated, I would have never developed the passion, desire, and resolve to dedicate myself and my family to making sure this business was a success.

We started our first business cleaning out foreclosed properties and getting them in marketable condition. We had done small jobs because we didn't have the money to hire any employees. I had done a few small jobs to build our income and get some cash coming in but my first big job was a huge house in a rural area that was owned by a hoarder. The house was absolutely loaded to the ceiling with trash. The bank wanted all the trash from this house out, loaded in dumpsters and taken away; I had three days to do it. They wanted all the trash, rat feces, car engines and dead animals taken out of this house. They also wanted every area of the house professionally deep cleaned so well you could eat off the floor. There was at least forty years of dirt and urine in this place. I said to myself, "You can't shine a turd." The reality was I had to do it if I wanted to stay in business. I was not only going to have to shine a turd, but I was going to have to carry a rusty car engine, an old rusty lawn mower, and a beat up plow blade about 200 feet from the enormous back yard to the dumpsters; which we had to place in the side yard. I had my wife to help with some trash and the deep cleaning but the heavy stuff was on me.

The thought of having to meet this deadline with just the two of us almost had me in tears. I nearly cried until I thought about the occupation I was trying to get away from; feeling nervous or like I was going to lose my job every day. I was afraid to drink water because if I stopped my machine to use the bathroom the supervisor might lay me off. I thought about never being able to take a vacation. I thought about running an excavator and the supervisor timing me to see who the fastest operator was because the slower guy would get laid off. I remembered being sick in the morning and throwing up because I was stressed out and didn't know if I could keep my job long enough to pay off some pressing bills.

I thought about all the crap I had been through trying to keep my job and take care of my family. Then I thought about owning my own business and never having to be abused by another heartless employer again, and I happily packed three, thirty yard dumpsters; lawnmower, car engines, doghouses, chicken coups, mattresses, refrigerators, dead animal feces and all. I did it with a smile on my face because this seemed like easy work compared to the crap I had to put up with in the industry I had left.

Maybe the pain in your life is preparing you for something magnanimous God is going to do for you. God allowed us to go down to our last 21 dollars before he touched our business because he wanted to show us that it wasn't our money or ability that built the company but only his miraculous power could bring us out. All along the way of our sufferings God was there setting us up for a blessing and if we had known at the time we would have felt better about the trials we had to go through. How many trials have we gone through in our life and thought it was the end of the world for us? I must say countless trials. God is always faithful in bringing us out of every situation better, wiser, smarter, and stronger than we went in. If we have faith in God we can have peace through every difficult period or battle in our life. When you know God is setting you up and all things are working together for your good, you don't have to worry.

When I look back over my life at some of the situations I went through and at the time I contemplated taking my own life, God brought me out and blessed me as a result of the situation. The situation wasn't good, but it worked out for my good. I can smile about it now and say like the apostle Paul, "It was good for me that I had been afflicted." If I had known at the time how God was going to bring me out I would have been able to have peace in the situation. Nothing we go through in Christ can hurt us because God is just setting us up for a blessing and we can have peace knowing that God is always for us. The word peace in English according to Webster means the absence of war. The word peace in the bible has a much different meaning. It comes from a Hebrew word Shalom which is not the absence of war but health, prosperity, comfort and assured victory even in war. Hebrew 10:38 says, "the just shall live by faith." If you want to live in the peace of God, just have faith that your victory is guaranteed in Christ.

The suffering of your past strengthens you and gives you the passion you need to fight your way into your destiny. Trials make it easy to persevere through the difficulties you must endure to fight your way into your destiny because they wane in comparison to what you've already had to fight through. The bible tells us to rejoice when we come into trials and temptations (James 1:2). Those trials strengthen you to handle the pressures and battles you need to fight in order to become successful in life.

Some people allow negative situations to destroy them and move them into a state of depression and hopelessness but someone else will take that same situation and use it as fuel to accomplish great things in their life. Just like in a stew, the same hot water that makes the potato soft will also make the meat tougher. The difference between success and failure is how you handle the heat. Your hardships are designed to make you better not bitter. Every layoff is just an opportunity to start a new job or open a business if you see it as an opportunity. Know that God is teaching you something in every trial and preparing something better for you because he said no good thing will I withhold from you (Psalms 84:11). Trust God in your trials, I've learned that you'll win if you don't quit.

LEGACY

"Most assuredly, I say to you, he who believes in me, the works that I do he will do also; and greater works than these he will do, because I go to My Father."

John 14:12

Many of us think of legacy as being a large financial inheritance. Legacy is so much more than that. Lots of people get rich, burn through the money and die broke. When this happens, it is a clear indication that these people missed the skills required to build legacy. Legacy is the establishment of generational blessings. Generational blessings are good characteristics, morals, wealth, and life building principles that are handed down from those that precede us in life. Generational blessings are designed to pass down life's lessons so that the next generation can start their journey off where the previous generation left off; continuing to improve the craft. Essentially, God designed the principle of generational blessing so that the next generation can create a stronger, wiser, and more fruitful life than that of the previous one. The obligation of the recipient is to continue to develop what was given using their uniqueness, updating with innovation deepened knowledge and improvements. Everything is a usable resource to continue with; money, morals, points of view and buildings. It's all for development, growth and expansion of the next generation.

Some of us have had a negative legacy handed down to us. We can easily get stuck in a generational rut and continue in mindsets with principles that are self destructive when you don't embrace a different perspective; like God's principles for wealth. The types of generational curses that can be handed down to us are: negative thinking patterns, debt, bitterness, seeing yourself as little, insecurities, and feelings of inadequacy, just to name a few. We have to break out of negative patterns and ideologies in order to achieve the success that God has for us.

After the civil war many slaves were given the opportunity to leave their plantations but they stayed because that was all they knew. They weren't taught to take risks; having stability, "three hots and a cot," were the best standards a former slave could have hoped for. They were even willing to put up with bondage in order to achieve it. They weren't handed down privilege, they were handed down oppression.

If oppression and ignorance are all you know then it becomes normal to you. Whatever you're used to becomes your normal. The longer you stay in that mindset the more generations develop in it, and the more normal it becomes to the detriment of your legacy. People become comfortable in the traditions and lifestyle that they live in and even when they are offered freedom they return to what is normal for them.

We develop negative thinking patterns that are adaptive in helping us survive in an abusive environment; whatever we live in becomes normal for us. We adapt ourselves to that environment because it has become normal and in looking at the world from this perspective will pass these same mindsets on to others that we mentor in our lives. Our children will use our thinking patterns for selecting a spouse or boyfriend. Our children tend to have the marriage they saw in their house. If we accept abuse, they are more likely to accept abuse. Like any other tradition, the principles and skills we have developed in life are passed along to others; it's not just our kids that we pass it along to. It is also the people we encounter in life that are recipients of our influence. We transfer and affect those around us with our normal.

As a descendant of slavery I understand that the principles, ignorance, settling for less, and normality of abnormal situations are handed down from generation to generation. In an article by Quatrus Carr, he describes how many slaves remained on plantations after slavery was abolished and the civil war was over as share croppers(Carr, 2016). My understanding of this time was that many slave masters rounded up their slaves and gave them a speech about how there are no opportunities out there in the world for them and if they want a stable secure environment they should stay on the plantation.

This similar speech seems to be handed down to many modern families today, "Stay where you are," or "The devil you know is better than the devil you don't know," and so on.

It was inconceivable for the slaves to dream of a better life away from the plantation. Slavery was normal to them and there were many negative mindsets and belief systems causing them to lack belief in themselves and their ability to become successful on their own. It was especially ignorant for those that could become entrepreneurs not to take the opportunity even though they knew every aspect of business from having run it for their masters. What they knew in slavery had become normal to many slaves and they could remain in their normal stable environment with a more tolerant master who was less abusive and would only beat them if they really deserved it. This was an exciting improvement compared to what they had before so many slaves stayed on their plantations rather than venture out into the unknown.

Our bodies respond to normality as well. For example, if slamming a rock in my hand becomes a daily activity I allow myself to experience, my hand will develop a callous in an adaptive response to being struck. Eventually I will become more comfortable with the normality of the abuse. If I miss a day of abusing my hand, I will develop an itchy, throbbing sensation that yearns for the abuse to happen because it's comfortable in what has been introduced as normal. So no matter how dysfunctional or abusive your living arrangement might be, if you stay there you will not only adapt but will also be drawn towards a negative normality. We become comfortable in a situation that would make others cringe. We willingly put ourselves in situations that are damaging and abusive to us. We leave good opportunities for bad ones, break up with good boyfriends for abusive ones, move from freedom to a different form of slavery because we become comfortable in normal and if abuse is normal then abuse is what we move to.

As a human tendency, we move towards normal and familiar rather than take the risk of venturing into an unknown territory. After many years of oppression, being emasculated and mentally torn down, slaves didn't believe they were good enough to achieve anything better than what they were used to. They put themselves in bondage situations because bondage was what they were used to. They couldn't see better for themselves than what they were used to. They overlooked the visions and dreams that God gave them because they were little in their own eyes. The legacy and principles of slavery were handed down instead of Gods legacy and wealth building principles.

Today people have the same mindsets. Remaining at a job that pays you just enough to keep your head above water but doesn't pay you enough to get you out of a hole, and forfeits your divine legacy. Dreaming dreams of a nice home, vacations, paying college tuition for your children, helping the poor

". . . the works that I do he will do also; and greater works than these he will do, because I go to My Father."

John 14:12

and needy, will not build your legacy. Using God's principles concerning success will.

I too was limited in my ability to believe that I had more options than what I grew up seeing. I never thought I could be an entrepreneur because the best I could have hoped for was getting a stable job that I didn't really like and dragging myself out of bed to get to it every morning.

It wasn't until I got around successful people of other backgrounds, ethnicities and upbringings that I began to see new normals and world views based on principles that were handed down to successful progressive people; the results were staggering. It wasn't until I started my union job operating heavy equipment that I began to see the byproduct of so many solid and progressive legacies of my own.

I was twenty two years old, newly married and looking for a good paying job when I found out what an operating engineer was. My father told me that my grandfather was the first black operating engineer in Massachusetts. I asked, "what's an operating engineer?" He explained, "Oh! They operate cranes, bulldozers, excavators, and they also fix them." I had about one more year of college before I would graduate as a special education teacher and after doing internships and college work at a few schools I knew I was going to hate that job. My father wasn't crazy about his teaching jobs either, but the steady paycheck and his responsibility to his family were what kept him there. I saw this union job as a way out of the occupation I was headed towards; it held the opportunity to do something I might enjoy; to do something that might build on to my legacy.

I was accepted into the operating engineer program and I really enjoyed the work. I would be paired up with different heavy equipment operators as an apprentice to learn all the skills that were required for me to become a successful operating engineer. I was never bored because I didn't stay on any job for very long. I would be on a tower crane for two weeks, an excavator for several months, and I would be in a mechanics truck going from job to job fixing everyone's equipment and assembling cranes. I loved the excitement of being on heavy equipment and moving around to new jobs.

Moving around on so many different jobs gave me the opportunity to work with a lot of different people. We would spend 12 to 16 hours a day with each other working, laughing and learning from each other. Most of the members were Irish or Italian. Many of them were 2nd, 3rd and 4th generation operating engineers. Some of the people I worked with were very racist and world class a…holes but many of the operators were some of the most wonderful thoughtful people I have ever met. We spent a lot of time together so many of us became very good friends.

As I was being taught and mentored by these operators I noticed some recurring themes. Many of the great attributes I admired about these great men led back to family. I heard stories of things handed down from parents, grandparents, great grandparents and even great, great grandparents. Everyone had the highest level of work ethic that I had ever encountered. They had the biblical work ethic that

Christians should have of working hard like your working for God.

"Work willingly at whatever you do, as though you were working for the Lord rather than for people." (Colossians 3:23)

They would be on the job ready to work 1 to 2 hours early. When I would ask them how they developed their work ethic they would give me responses like, " my father always told me if you ain't a half an hour early then you're late," or,"...my dad said be early to work just in case you get a flat tire on the way; you need enough time to fix the flat so you're not late." I also noticed how highly skilled they were at their jobs. I found that the operators that were second generation were amazing in their ability. Most of them were learning this from their fathers who owned construction companies or worked on farms when they were kids. The average guy off the street could never compete with these guys in terms of skill because there were handed down tips and pointers going back three generations.

". . . the works that I do he will do also; and greater works than these he will do, because I go to My Father."

John 14:12

I noticed something else about them, many of them had businesses, and I don't mean small businesses. One had a logging company in Maine with a couple million dollars worth of logging equipment. Some had owned their own million dollar construction companies, cashed in on the business and were only working to keep from being bored. Many owned pizza shops, crane rentals services, repair shops, carpentry businesses, investment firms, stores, restaurants, big farms with government contracts, and everything you can think of. Almost everyone had at least two streams of income. Everything kept pointing back to their family; these skills were handed down to them. Not only had most of their parents taught them amazing skill, but many of them left money and houses for them. Some members were selling land their fathers had bought and collecting million dollar checks on. Some would lose a relative and inherit two houses, some would retire early because they decided to sell their business and retire. When someone died there was always a hefty insurance policy and even though people were taking up collections for the family I heard one guy say, "We're not accepting any more money." I have never heard anyone say this. I'm used to seeing people die and they're trying to raise money just to bury the person and the family is left with more bills than they already had. This was amazing but totally foreign to me because most of the kids I had grown up with didn't have family legacies like these. Some handed down legacies of drug addiction, violence, spousal abuse, and gang culture.

God has created us with such greatness that it would be a shame if at the end of our lives we left this earth with all of the wisdom and blessings we acquired in this life. It is our duty to leave something behind for those that come after us; legacy as shared in John 14:12, "Most assuredly, I say to you, he who believes in Me, the works that I do he will do also; and greater works than these he will do, because I go to My Father." The sign of a good legacy is that we create a greater work than what our ancestors did. Those that follow us can take the gift they have, take up where we left off, combine what they have with all that we pour into them and create a more powerful and effective work than what we did. We can replicate and improve on our gifts, abilities and wisdom many times over in those that we mentor. Real legacy is not letting what God has given us die, but multiplying it in those we mentor.

REDEFINING SUCCESS

"Now godliness with contentment is great gain."

1 Timothy 6:6

Success is a relative term depending on who you are and what you are looking to achieve. However, everyone who envisions success and the peace that it will bring does it similarly. We all have different goals or vocations that we aspire to. No matter the goal, we associate the attaining of our goal with a feeling of fulfillment, accomplishment, and peace. We have an idea in our heads when we set out to accomplish our goal and what we will feel like when we arrive at our destination. For many people they arrive at the destination they set out for and while they land exactly where they intended and accomplish what they wanted, they realize it doesn't do for them what they had expected. Success is so much more than simply meeting a mark.

We are looking for so much more than just attaining a goal when we envision success. Everyone wants to be successful in life and I believe that desire for success is developed in all of us as children. Children are so innocent and free from the pressures of this world. When I get overwhelmed with adulthood I reflect back on my childhood experiences; a time when the joys of peace and family love molded my understanding of what is most important in life.

Old movies and programs helped shape my world view and the definition of who I am as a Christian man. I loved to watch "I love Lucy," "Different Strokes," "Woody Woodpecker," "Popeye the Sailor Man," "Archie Bunker," "Welcome Back Cotter," "Grizzly Adams," The Dukes of Hazard," and my all time favorite, "Starsky and Hutch."

The depictions of my favorite characters on television became the characters I aspired to become like. Our understanding of success was molded by our environmental influences. The influential characters on TV depicted success, but were their depictions truly a reality? Like me, many spent their entire childhood basing who we want to become and what success looks like off of television shows but is that what it was really like?

Many of us grew up watching military, family, and police shows and we remember them as the happiest days of our life. The impressions they gave us about the joys of being a police officer and playing police officer with our little toy guns and handcuffs stick with us all the way into our adult life. Children don't understand the implications of wearing a real badge or shooting a real gun. They think of the fantasy and the joy that they felt in wearing the toy badge, but after working in a police department they would understand it's not at all like they imagined as a child.

In life we tend to look at the finished product of a job or position without weighing the total cost of donning the position. We look at everything on the surface and make the determination that this is what I want without knowing what it really means. We have our views shaped in life by popular TV shows and influences that only portray the external and attractive pieces. And while we live out our fantasies as these television characters, We don't know the real implications that are associated with the character because it's not at all like we imagined as a child.

Nobody at elementary age says, "I want to be depressed and shoot a heroin needle in my arm until it eventually kills me." But they will aspire to be the drug dealer they see on the corner that drives a nice car and buys children ice cream cones. No child aspiring to be a police officer says, "I want to do a thankless job and have thoughts of suicide at the end of my workday." But they want to be like magnum P.I. or Will Smith in Bad Boys. No little girl says, "I want to argue with my children and feel unfulfilled in my marriage." But they look at the happiest wife not knowing what it's like to walk a day in her shoes. As children we make exciting fulfilling characterizations of who we want to become.

For this reason, it is important to clearly define success because if we haven't defined it, how will we know when we've arrived. When asked to define success I've heard people use phrases like "whatever success means to you" or "however you determine when you are successful." We must redefine success based on the characterization of what we actually envision and not just a dictionary definition because we can attain the letter definition of success and completely miss the spirit of what we are trying to attain.

Dictionary.com defines success as the accomplishment of one's goal and the attainment of wealth position honors, or the like. In our pursuit of success what is the essence of what we are looking for? When we endeavor to be successful we envision success as so much more than simply attaining a goal. When we think of being successful there is a characterization or vision of success that we see. We see a portrayal of success that encompasses happiness, inner peace, contentment, freedom from any form of bondage, freedom to do or accomplish whatever we set out to do, as well as the acquisition of wealth and honor.

Success can't simply be accomplishments because there are so many intangibles that are wrapped up in success. In fact I've grown to learn that the intangibles of success are much more important to any success than the acquisitions of the tangible. "Now godliness with contentment is great gain" (1 Timothy 6:6).

What good is the acquisition of a beautiful wife with a miserable marriage? What good is a million dollar house that doesn't feel like home? How can one say that they are successful after having achieved honors, wealth and power but when they are alone they put a gun in their mouth and struggle to find a reason to keep living? It is the intangibles of success that make success sweet. The freedom to acquire things and positions is great but you can't buy the intangibles of success with all the money in the world. In fact, you can be dead broke and still be richly fulfilled.

The intangibles of success are sought out by everyone from every walk of life. There is a restlessness that is in us searching for something that we cannot see and we look to satisfy that void through relationships, drugs, accomplishments, and acquisitions but our pursuit of temporal things only frustrates us more in life. You can be blinded by a new relationship and when the excitement of the new relationship wears off you are back at square one. The bible says Godliness with contentment is great gain.

(1 Timothy 6:6) so we must seek fist the things of God and then the tangible blessings will be enjoyable (Matthew 6:33).

Success is a journey and not a destination because God is process driven, not result driven. God is not impressed with the destination you arrive at but he is more impressed with how you got there. We couldn't enter a car race, take a shortcut through the track, run over four people and count the race a successful win just because we crossed the finish line before everybody else. Success can't simply be the attaining of one's goal, reaching the finish line. There is a process that must be adhered to. People who are successful can relate to each other because they have gone through similar journeys. They fought similar fights, different vocations but similar struggles. Acquisition of a goal can be ill gotten but ill gotten success is not only fleeting, (Proverbs 13:11) but wealth gained by dishonesty will be diminished. He who gathers by labor will increase. Proverbs 10:2 Treasures of wickedness profit nothing, but righteousness delivers from death. Proverbs 11:18 Evil people get rich for the moment, but the reward of the godly will last.

We can be so focused on acquiring wealth that we neglect the creator and the God that causes us to prosper. We should remember that the blessings of the lord make us rich but we lose sight of the more important fact that he adds no sorrow with it. We can get lost in the acquisition of the created thing to the point where we take shortcuts acting outside of our integrity; we lose sight of God's purpose, estranging ourselves and losing the joy, peace and relationship that the money was only meant to enhance in bringing us closer to our God. Money is great and while the main purpose of money is for God's work we also can enjoy fun and reap benefits of it. But we must remember that everything on earth is temporal and what we do on earth has everlasting benefits and repercussions. The real treasures are in heaven and they are based on what we do here on earth.

"Now godliness with contentment is great gain."
1 Timothy 6:6

"For we must all appear before the judgment seat of Christ, that each one may receive the things done in the body, according to what he has done, whether good or bad." (2 Corinthians 5:10)

"For we brought nothing into this world, and it is certain we can carry nothing out." (1 Timothy 6:7)

We must be focused on the most important things in life that will yield an eternal and undying result. We should lay up treasures in heaven. "Do not lay up for yourselves treasures on earth, where moth and rust destroy and where thieves break in and steal; but lay up for yourselves treasures in heaven, where neither moth nor rust destroys and where thieves do not break in and steal. For where your treasure is, there your heart will be also" (Matthew 6:19-21).

God is not concerned with the acquisition of things; he is concerned with having relationship with you and taking you through the process in life that brings you closer to him so that when you acquire the success, you can enjoy the fullness and depth of a win in God. There is a purpose behind our successes in life. God wants a relationship with us and he wants us to learn some things through the process. We cannot miss the joys of the journey because our vision is set on the end result. The result alone won't bring the joys because the joy is in the relationship, and lesson learned through the journey. It's not a blessing if God didn't give it and it's not success if it didn't come through his process.

"The blessing of the Lord makes me rich, and He adds no sorrow with it" (Proverbs 10:22).

'Blessings,' in the bible is an all encompassing declaration. In the Greek especially, you can see that blessing means so much more than money or accomplishments alone. There are many Greek words for the word blessing; Makarios which means happy and fortunate in receiving provision from God. Eulogia, which means to praise or speak well of. God speaks well of you and is proud of you like Job who he spoke well of. All of God's blessings involve peace and provision. God's blessings are a declaration of faith that encompasses success in our endeavors as well as the joys, peace and faith to know that if it hasn't happened yet, it's on the way." God who calls those thing that are not as though they were " (Romans 4:17) makes declarations in our life and gives us authority to make declarations; he expects us to count ourselves successful because we believe the promises of God and as we move into the great things that God has for us we enjoy every element of blessing as we progress. As joy comes, we rejoice, as peace comes we rejoice, as healing comes, we rejoice, as money comes, we rejoice, as relationships heal, we rejoice, as marriages strengthen, we rejoice. As we set out to pursuit the vision and purpose God places in our heart we know we have what we ask of him.

"And we are confident that he hears us whenever we ask for anything that pleases him. And since we know he hears us when we make our requests, we also know that he will give us what we ask for" (1 John 5:15-15).

My wife and I built our family business from $21.00 to $2 million in revenue annually. We are successful but the success is not in the dollar amount. The dollar amount is just a byproduct of God showing the world what he can do with two kids from the hood, $21 bucks, and a will to serve him. We were successful through God's provision and his purpose for our lives.

We kept our family together in God, we loved each other, we learned from each other, and all the troubles, trials and triumphs worked together for our good in molding us into the people of God that God called us to be; for this reason the journey was successful. We counted ourselves successful when we were in the dirty basement of a pizza shop praying for an opportunity and trying to figure out how to make ends meet. We were successful when our children willingly took all their pennies and brought them to us so we could get our last 21 dollars to start a business. We were successful when I had tears in my eyes because I couldn't provide for my family and my wife kissed me and said I believe in you. We were successful when our children laid their hands on us and prayed for our family and our business.

"Now godliness with contentment is great gain."
1 Timothy 6:6

We were successful years later when God grew our construction business from that $21 dollars into a $2 million dollar annual business. We were successful when I used God's biblical principles to develop a construction field team that was able to successfully complete 40 to 52 projects a month without my constant tutelage. We were also successful years later when we were vacationing in Puerto Rico while our business in MA was making money. God is a God of process and because his promises are true no matter where you are in life, count yourself blessed. Don't miss the joys of the journey but enjoy the journey knowing that you will attain the goal. Success is found in the purpose and journey God destined for you. The biggest impediment to your success is yourself.

WORLDLY DOMINANCE/THE KOSMOS

"Casting down arguments and every high thing that exalts itself against the knowledge of God, bringing every thought into captivity to the obedience of Christ."

2 Corinthians 10:5

You must cast down imaginations and arguments. Everything created started with a thought. Every great battle is fought first in the mind. What originates as a thought is carried out to fruition and can be seen as a manifestation in the natural. Nothing is created without first being a thought. My wife and I's biggest obstacles in building a million dollar company came from our minds.

All battles are fought and won in the mind. Spiritual warfare is fought in the mind and the condition and state of the earth is a result of many battles in the minds of people. War, terrorism, famine and poverty are not the battle; they are the after effect and end result of a battle that was lost in the mind.

Every spiritual battle arises from an ideological thought that keeps people unproductive, broke and robs people of their rightful dominion and power on earth. The battle is in the mind and the control over our ways of thinking; our thought processes and how we process the information we see and hear. The most critical and fierce spiritual battles are not waged in casting demons out of people, or in creaks in the middle of the night but rather in casting down imaginations and arguments of the mind.

The real battle is in the minds of the people; spiritual warfare is fought in the mind. A demon doesn't really care about controlling one person as much as he cares about controlling entire regions; a thief to legacy. He works to control the mind through the media, television, radio and the systems that govern how people think. There are three common doctrines of demons in the modern church:

Deception - Satan works to deceive God's people with demonic doctrines that prevent God's people from pursuing the building of wealth for God's purposes.

Narcissism - Living a totally selfish narcissistic life of opulence and excess without any regard for God's purposes.

Impotent/Sins of Omission - There are doctrines and ideologies that keep God's people impotent and unable to do God's work because they are prevented by religious customs and traditions that are not biblical teaching the people of God that being unproductive is not a sin.

> "Don't let anyone capture you with empty philosophies
> and high-sounding nonsense that come from human thinking
> and from the spiritual powers of this world, rather than from
> Christ." (Colossians 2:8) "Now the Spirit expressly says that
> in latter times some will depart from the faith, giving heed to
> deceiving spirits and doctrines of demons," (1 Timothy 4:1).

Demons want to creep into our thinking processes and deceive us into believing a false form of godliness that leads us to destruction. Satan always uses a little bit of scripture but changes a small point so it leads to corruption.

Demons teach ideologies like love yourself which has great biblical truth in it but if followed up by a world system that reinforces it with self centered ideologies can be used to developing a selfish narcissistic society that emphasizes only self love excluding love of others. Those affected by the Kosmos can become so self-absorbed that loving others is not possible because all emphasis and energy is placed only on love of oneself. The principle of denying oneself and selflessness; like the way Jesus lived, are precepts that we should live by so the ideologies of this world that are aimed at opposing the ideologies of our faith will not breed. We must form our spirituality through the word of God. Be careful in receiving worldly philosophies from secular sources because while many have good points, the world system is crafty, in putting it's corrupting ideologies into good philosophies. We must weigh everything against the word of God for its usefulness in our lives. Our combat against this is the word of God. The word of God will permeate our thoughts as we read it and God's Holy Spirit will reinforce the correct thought process in us.

We must take captive every thought and philosophy that enters our mind through television, radio, Internet, books and even our own thought life. We cannot be influenced by this world; we were called to influence. God's word is the template for good appropriate thoughts that will move us into our destiny in Christ and rebuke negative thoughts that the enemy plants through his deceptive philosophies and teachings.

THE KOSMOS

"Do not love the world or the things in the world. If anyone loves the world, the love of the Father is not in him."

1 John 2:15

God gave us dominion on earth in the Garden of Eden. God gave us all the instructions, principles and gifts we needed to maintain that dominion. He even gave mankind a help meet in the form of a woman and said let them (both Adam and Eve) have dominion together as equals in value but having different roles in terms of leadership and position. He gave us all authority on earth as ambassadors for him so that when we speak we speak with the authority of God as his mouthpiece.

Whatever we do or produce, we produce it in the name of our God as full representatives of the kingdom of heaven. Now somewhere between God giving us this world and mankind leaving the Garden of Eden, Satan took control of this world. God's gifts come without repentance and he doesn't take his gifts away from us so we still have the dominion and authority that he gave us on earth however, Jesus called Satan the ruler of this world. (John 14:30, John 12:31) All through scripture we hear about the world being evil and being controlled by Satan. 1 John 2:15 says, "Do not love the world or the things in the world. If anyone loves the world, the love of the Father is not in him." James 4:4 says, "You adulterous people! Do you not know that friendship with the world is enmity with God? Therefore whoever wishes to be a friend of the world makes himself an enemy of God."

". . . If anyone loves the world, the love of the Father is not in him."

1 John 2:15

Our understanding of dominating this earth, taking authority, and being blessed on earth as we live out the principles of God on earth can be really confusing. To further confuse our understanding of God's perspective of this world we have another scripture that seems to totally contradict what God just said about the world. John 3:16 says, "For God so loved the world, that he gave his only Son, that whoever believes in him should not perish but have eternal life."

One scripture is talking about how God so loved the world and the other scripture is telling us not to love the world. The Bible talks about

God so loved the world and then you can find him vacillating between two scriptures about the world saying, love of the world is hatred towards God and do not love the world. What does this mean? In order to get a full understanding of what appears to be major contradictions you must understand the original Greek text.

The Greek language is very descriptive and there are two different words that are being used for the word 'world.' First there is "God so loved the world." The word 'world' used here is one that we are all very familiar with. It represents God's creation and the people that fill it, the system and kingdoms on earth. This is the world that God gave us to have authority over and to dominate.

The alternate meaning of the word 'world' is a Greek word called Kosmos. This word means a world system that Satan created to be hostile towards God (Bible Hub, 2016). The word Kosmos literally and actually means a system that is purposely created in hatred towards God bent towards blasphemy and intended to destroy the things of God. The Kosmos is a world system and a world order. The word Kosmos is derived from the verb Kosmien which is a military word for organizing troops for battle. It means to be organized, deliberate and strategic in waging war and total destruction of one's enemy. The Kosmos is the calculated militaristic system of hostility toward God designed to overthrow God and the people of God (Bible Study Tools, 2016). To understand how this war is waged and what system is hostile towards God we have to look at Romans 8:6-8, "For to set the mind on the flesh is death, but to set the mind on the Spirit is life and peace."

The mind that is set on the flesh is hostile to God. It does not submit to God's law; indeed, it cannot. Those who are in the flesh cannot please God. The Kosmos is the system that affects our minds, our money, media, and every earthly system or kingdom in this world to bring it under subjection to Satan. Satan is stealing, killing and destroying the dominion and authority God gave to us (John 10:10). The thief; Satan, does not come except to steal, and to kill, and to destroy. But Jesus says, "I have come that they may have life, and that they may have it more abundantly." So how does Satan's Kosmos system dominate and rule? He rules the same way we should be ruling. He affects the hearts and minds of the people. He has financial dominance, that is, he makes lots of money. He controls the stock market, radio and television, sending subliminal messages that slowly affect our world view, how we see ourselves and how we see God. He replaces our good thoughts with negative and ungodly thoughts through television, radio, billboards, and video games. His financial dominance allows him the freedom to buy airtime and TV time to subliminally assert his agenda into the most entertaining programs. Financial dominance ensures he can hire the best movie directors and actors so that his programs are irresistible to all people.

If you listen to violent music you will begin to think more violently and even if you do not have a proclivity towards violent behaviors, over time you will become desensitized to violence and violence becomes more tolerable for you and society as a whole.

". . . If anyone loves the world, the love of the Father is not in him."

1 John 2:15

The Kosmos loads up television, billboards and media with sexual content. Over time we have become increasingly more sexually promiscuous as a society. Sexual themes that were formerly censored by Christian morals and were considered too offensive for network television have become an acceptable way of life. Sexy commercials become more tolerable. A television program like Scandal with an adulterous theme becomes not only tolerable but it begins to be accepted under certain conditions. "if the marriage wasn't that good anyway," "Their needs weren't being met anyway," are just some of the phrases that you might hear in support of accepting adultery as an excusable behavior. Before you know it the Kosmos captivates our desires for illicit sexuality and as a society dysfunctional behaviors are accepted and viewed as normal.

Over time these different forms of media begin to affect the minds and hearts of the people. The ideologies of the people are emulsified with the ideologies of the ruler of the world system through media. Media is such an influential tool that if the government wanted to encourage people to leave the city in order to alleviate congestion in the inner cities and populate areas that are virtually uninhabited all they would have to do is put television shows out about living in the wild. They could depict a portrayal of a clean and fulfilling lifestyles in different environments like Alaska, the Midwest, areas that need to be built up and you will see a tremendous explosion in tourism and population. If you take a frog and you try to put it in a pot of hot water it's going to jump out immediately but if you put it in the pot and warm up the water slowly you'll boil him to death. Getting control of the people's minds is just that way. Satan is very crafty in his attack. It's a strategic and subtle takeover, but it's very effective.

Whoever is in charge of the society, dictates what is normal. People begin to function in and under dysfunctional circumstances when dysfunction becomes normal. God originally created the environment and gave us the control over the media, finances, politics, government, etc. We are here to rule this earth, control and dominate. When that control was lost in the fall of Adam and Eve, the control of the earth went with it. We are here to control the systems and kingdoms of earth with the principles of Heaven. When living in purpose on purpose and dominating the cosmic presence of the world today, we have the power to expand the impact of earth to look like heaven in every area we touch; politics, government, music, finances and businesses. God never created us to inhabit a Kosmic environment any more than He created a fish to swim on land or a car to drive on the water. We must start creating the environment that God designed for us to live in. We must make our world conducive to kingdom living.

The Kosmos is dead set against God's values and seeks to create a world that is conducive to the affirmation and fulfillment of its own values; which are contrary in nature to the values of God. We as Christians have been given the keys (principles), authority and backing of our Heavenly Father who loves us. All we have to do is take back our authority as God commanded in every area of the earth by operating in our God given purpose on earth and executing his principles to assert our dominance on earth.

THE RESULTS OF THE KOSMOS

"Finally, brethren, whatever things are true, whatever things are noble, whatever things are just, whatever things are pure, whatever things are lovely, whatever things are of good report, if there is any virtue and if there is anything praiseworthy —meditate on these things."

Philippians 4:8

I remember a time in this country, when as a country children would pledge allegiance to the flag as one nation under God. The movies and programs at this time bore no inhibitions toward the mentioning of God and many of the themes in movies were designed to suggest morality and faith.

We watched movies like Where the Red Fern Grows which had themes of faith in God, hard work, and honesty. It's a movie about a poor young country boy who wanted a dog to help support his family by hunting coon hounds for meat and for the money. He learned that through prayer, faith and hard work he could achieve his dreams. There were other movies like, My Six Loves (1963), where a famous celebrity gave up her career to take care of six orphaned children. She learned that selflessness, love, purpose and fulfillment in life are more important than the accolades of stardom. This movie pointed back to the principles of God with themes of faith and family; the kids always prayed before bedtime, and restoring the children's faith in God's ability to provide for them was reinforced.

We weren't a perfect nation but at the time all throughout different media platforms, faith in God was a recurring theme. Many movies promoted faith, family and selflessness. The music at this time had more wholesome themes. The radio programs were not so aggressively dominated by the Kosmos; the world system that is hostile towards God. Back then Satan had a weaker hold on the media. There was no hostility at the mention of God in the media to influence our thinking and behaviors. Many of our influences were geared towards good and pleasant themes which promoted good and wholesome thoughts. The word of God says meditate on these things: "Finally, brethren, whatever things are true, whatever things are noble, whatever things are just, whatever things are pure, whatever things are lovely, whatever things are of good report, if there is any virtue and if there is anything praiseworthy—meditate on these things" (Philippians 4:8).

If there were themes in movies and media that were inappropriate, negative or hostile towards the ways of God there would be responses from the people of God fighting for a higher standard of morality because they realized that the media had profound effects on our culture and environment.

There was a popular movie released November 14th 1960 called the Facts of Life. This movie starring Bob Hope and Lucille Ball is about how two married friends get stranded at a hotel without their spouses. They were both frustrated with their marriages coupled with the opportunity to be intimate and the time alone weakened their already fragile emotional state. They fought the attraction for each other until their feelings became so strong they gave into the idea of having an affair. They went through great lengths of inconvenience to seal the deal of sleeping together but found no opportunity. They met for meals, went to the movies, reserved a cabin in the woods, but every time they met their plans for sin failed. Finally they were alone with the opportunity to carry out the affair and they came to themselves. They thought of their families at home, their spouses and everyone connected to them. The marriages they had weren't perfect. Their children depended on them and they had a responsibility to think of others instead of just thinking of themselves. They made the right decision and even though they had betrayed their families emotionally, they never followed through physically by having sex. They ended the affair before they took it to a place that they couldn't come back from.

This movie was a very controversial film at the time because of the themes of adultery. Many Christians were forbidden to watch this movie because of how controversial the subject of adultery in this film was. What is so jarring to me, having grown up in a different time where many forms of illicit sexuality is portrayed through media with no form of governing morality is, but they never even slept with each other! The film was condemned and banned by many religious groups at the time that same film today could be considered an inspirational film on the redemptive qualities of people who are tempted to make a bad decision and turn away before they get involved in a situation that they can't get out of. The same movie banned by churches in the 1960's can be used by churches today to portray a view of morality.

When a movie that was once considered controversial and taboo for Christians, can now be seen as an inspirational movie, and this is a sure sign of the continued moral decline in this country. Today we have television shows like Scandal where affairs are portrayed as justifiable because there is an emphasis to pamper and love oneself. If something is lacking in your relationship it is widely accepted that one should not have to deny oneself the feelings of the newness of an illicit relationship.

It's no secret that we are seeing a decline in morality and an upshot in crime, hatred, divorces, and trouble in the world. People are simply going through life without a purpose, agenda or any type of moral code. Everyone does what is right in their own eyes and there is no driving force behind why we are here on earth. I don't believe people have changed because people do what people do but society has changed. The world system, the environment has changed, and the Kosmos is getting stronger. Our earthly environment is becoming less conducive to holy living.

Like billions of people, I simply meandered through the earlier portion of my life. I went to work because that's what I was told to do. I went to college because that's what I was told to do. I hung out with people who I thought were fun to be around. I never got excited about much aside from good food or entertainment. I never had much passion about anything; nothing really woke me up early in the morning because I was excited about doing something really important that was going to make a difference in this world. I lived my life for myself. I was at the center and focal point of everything I did. Everything I did was centered on my happiness or my enjoyment. There was never a drive or an understanding for me to be involved in something greater than myself.

There are billions of people in this world who go through life the exact same way. They simply do things because that's what they are told they're supposed to do. When they wake up in the morning there is no drive to do something great. Most people don't even realize that there is greatness inside them. Everyone is preoccupied with themselves and because of that we live in a selfish world. We are susceptible to being caught up in any type of activity and lifestyle because we are not preoccupied with what God created us for and we get swept up into whatever environment we meander into.

Our world has become saturated with people who are self absorbed and their only purpose in life is to please themselves. When we come to the realization that there is a reason for our coming into being, our behavior begins to align itself with the purpose for our life. Our behaviors and choices must align themselves with the purpose for our lives.

Two very dangerous situations for us to be caught up into are a life without purpose and being in an environment that we were not created to be in. If you look around the world or even in your back yard you will notice an increase in violence, poverty, crime, broken homes and an overall decline in our society. At the rate of moral decline that we are heading in, the world will never last. This world was never created to be the way it is now. No society can continue and prosper the way our society is functioning today. If we want our society to last we must understand how to correct the issues in our society.

GOD'S ORIGINAL INTENTION

"So God created man in His own image, in the image of God He created him; male and female. He created them."

Genesis 1:27-30

To get back to God's original intention we all have to start using the skills and authority He gave to us, here on earth. Then we can maximize every opportunity on earth and really tap into the principles in the scriptures that help us to understand God's original intention regarding success, wealth, and legacy. God wants us to dominate, manage, prosper and rule the earth; replicating the character of God on earth.

"So God created man in His own image, in the image of God He created him; male and female. He created them."

Genesis 1:27-30

In order to understand that He made us like him to perpetuate his character we have to first understand why God wants us in his own likeness. The word likeness is used which means we are to be like God, we are to have the character of God, we are to emulate the behaviors and actions of God. So God created man and gave him a likeness after Him so that man would make decisions and manage the earth like God. Just like a restaurant franchise creates other franchises in its likeness, replicating the process and decisions on how to conduct business, God created man in his own likeness. When you go to any franchise restaurant you are getting the same product that you would get from the original but the character of the franchise remains the same. However the benefits are specific. The recipients of the franchise receive some benefits as a result of being under the franchise. Merriam Webster describes a franchise as, "a special privilege granted to an individual or group." What are some of the benefits of being associated with Gods franchise? You are given the association of his name. You are given God's dominion on earth. You are given his principles and precepts for success. You have a guaranteed formula for success and you have his protection.

Our success on earth is all about His original plan for us on this earth. God's original intention for us on earth was to spread the culture of heaven to the earth through the people of God, through strict adherence to the culture, and through principles and precepts of heaven. Remember the Lord's Prayer? "Thy kingdom come, thy will be done, on earth as it is in heaven." You have to know that 'Thy kingdom come,' is referring to us bringing the culture of heaven to earth, just like it is done in heaven.

WORKING TOGETHER
IN OUR OBLIGATION
TO PRODUCE WEALTH

"Economic power is a very formidable force; with lots of money you can get just about anything accomplished."

In 1921 in Tulsa Oklahoma under the oppressive Jim Crow segregation laws there was a very affluent and independent town that affectionately became known as Black Wall Street (PBS, 2002). During this time in 1921 it was unfathomable for people of color to own property, a business, to be educated or progress in any way because blacks were not given equal rights. There were many people of color who had experienced slavery and being free was an overwhelming but appreciated change for many people of color. The thought of owning a business or being educated was inconceivable for most people of color. Oklahoma was a vast and uninhabited area where many Native Americans relocated when their land was taken from them.

Many African Americans were allowed to claim land in this region which was a very attractive for many African Americans who were former slave and children of former slaves. The black population in this area grew and with the growth there was a need for stores, transportation, doctors, lawyers, construction and all the amenities of life. Under the Jim Crow segregation laws blacks were not allowed to live in town or shop in town and with the problem of no places to live or the amenities of life, people of color had no choice but to create their own stores and businesses. Blacks began to start businesses and a very prosperous city was created. That city became affectionately known as Black Wall Street.

Black Wall Street became a 36 square block business district with over 600 businesses. It housed about 15,000 black residents where the dollar was believed to have circulated 36 to 100 times before it left the community. There were 21 churches, 21 restaurants, 30 grocery stores, 2 movie theaters, a hospital, a bank, a post office, libraries, schools, law offices, private airplanes, and a bus system. Everything was black owned and the amount of wealth was astronomical for these people. One report stated that a Dr. Berry who owned the bus system earned $500 a day which was an astronomical amount of money in the 1920's. There were educated people from many different trades and professions. This was a God fearing powerful black and independent community in a very racist and hostile state. There was talk of electing a black Governor and as their money grew, so did their power and influence. At their rate of economic growth they could have become a dominant financial political and international power. The world would have to listen to them because the world understands the influence of money. You cannot oppress a people with a powerful political and economic power. You cannot oppress a person you may need to borrow money from. When you own a bank, a transportation company, stores or you sell the best lumber in town, anyone who needs your product must treat you with a certain level of dignity or they won't get the product they want. Financial power leads to political power. Whoever gets elected has the ability to change the policies and assert the will of their group. Money pays for good campaigns which aid in getting people elected. The money that was generated in this town was the key to equality and a voice in politics as well as at the bargaining table. With wealth, black people finally had the ability to change their standing in

"Economic power is a very formidable force; . . .

society and become equals with whites but their growing economic power did not go unnoticed. The Klan members and racist citizens of Oklahoma understood that their independence and financial power would allow them the freedom to become equals and have an equal say in governing the direction of our country so a plan was devised to stop the economic progress of Black Wall Street.

On June 1,1921 a white woman fabricated a false rape allegation against a black man who tripped and bumped into her in an elevator. The falsified claim was never looked into, the woman didn't move forward with the prosecution because it was totally fabricated. The rape allegations were just the excuse the racist people of Oklahoma needed to converge on this thriving town, destroy these business and murder innocent victims. In the span of about 12 hours 300 black people were murdered in cold blood and over 600 businesses were either vandalized or burned to the ground. Racist Whites destroyed African Americans economic power because it was the key to receiving justice and equality.

Economic power is a very formidable force; with lots of money you can get just about anything accomplished. As people of God we should have economic power. We can pattern ourselves after the people of Black Wall Street and circulate the Christian dollars within our own communities. God has designed for his people to work together in bringing about his purpose in life. The world system (Kosmos) does not have a problem with us going to church every Sunday and having an emotional experience every week, but when God's people become a dominant financial power, we can expect problems. When we run politics, media and have influence in this world we will begin to get resistance from the world because we can become the dominant force in this world. Just like the KKK didn't want the colored people of Oklahoma developing into a dominant financial power, Satan's Kosmos doesn't want to give up control of the world system but we have the authority and power issued by God to take back dominion on earth and run the earth the way God originally intended. We can develop into a powerful world influence and take back the authority that God gave us in the beginning. Christians can re-circulate the Christian dollar throughout the Christian community, tithing back to God's house for good work.

We don't have to be dependent on worldly television and radio stations that are hostile towards God's belief systems when we can create our own programs that perpetuate God's agenda. We have the ability to control our environment but we have to have the financial power and influence to do it. With money and influence we don't have to ask for favors but with money and influence we can demand God's agenda be upheld. We have a responsibility to take back authority on earth. Just like the people on Black Wall Street were attacked, we as Christians might be attacked or deterred in some way because the fight to get back in position takes power away from Satan's Kosmos. But if God be for us, He is more than the whole world against us.

In the book, *The Jewish Phenomenon* by Steve Silbiger, it outlines the principles behind the success of the Jewish people. Jewish people dominate in power and influence in many areas of American society which is startling when you consider that numerically they are amongst the least represented of all minority groups, (Silbiger, 2000). Despite the, they have the money and influence to demand change. They keep their influence because they make sure that as a culture they pour money back into their culture. Jewish people support Jewish business.

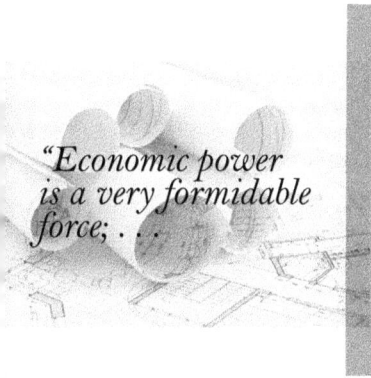

"Economic power is a very formidable force; . . ."

As Christians we must do a better job of keeping Christian money in the Christian culture. Why not support businesses and people that align with our Christian agenda? Every dollar we spend in the world just strengthens the world, but we can grow stronger and more influential when we support ourselves. God's money is for His purposes so we must be mindful of where we allocate such a valuable and influential resource.

MANagement

"The heavens are the LORD'S heavens, but the earth he has given to the children of mankind."

Psalm 115:16

Take a look at the ecology of the earth. Nothing was created without a purpose. God never created anything without a specific purpose in mind. Even our ecological system is so intricately designed that even the removal of one animal or sequence could send entire regions into total chaos. From every piece of fuzz on a peach to the smallest bacteria; from the largest of mammals to the smallest micro organism, God created everything with a purpose. Ducks were created with an oil gland near their tail; the ducks spread the oil on the top layer of their feathers to repel water so that when they swim their outer feathers keep the inner feathers warm and dry. They are designed for their environment and they have a perfect role and purpose in it. Even the dung of animals has a purpose. We call dung waste but nothing is wasted. Every part of the dung has a use. Animal dung is used as seed starters; food for insects and microorganism, fertilizer, not even the smallest dropping is wasted or created without a critical and specific purpose in our ecosystem. The way that plants are shaped has purpose, the scent of a skunk has purpose, the scentless nature of a baby doe; which keeps them from being detected by predators and allows them time to grow has purpose; God has a purpose behind everything.

God created us to dominate and manage the earth; to perpetuate the culture of heaven on earth; to dwell prosperously in that environment. What happens when the people of God remove themselves; through inactivity of purpose, from the delicately balanced ecology of the world system that God created? The ecology of the world system is thrown into chaos. We may not be removed as humans, but if we are removed as an active presence in the world by neglecting the divine order for managing the earth, we are removed none the less. By not dominating and setting systems in place, by not possessing political powers, influence, controlling the environment and leading the world with the principles of God, we have rendered ourselves an endangered species.

Let's talk about man-agement. God designed us in such a way that when we discover our purpose on earth and become actively engaged in doing what he created us to do, we are man-aging the earth; dominating it and saturating the earth with the good culture of heaven. Man is created for man-agement; man is God's answer for keeping order on earth.

As God was creating earth he retarded growth until he was sure order would be upheld. Dr. Myles Monroe, exegesis from the book Genesis 2:5 reads, "Neither wild plants nor grains were growing on the earth. For the Lord God had not yet sent rain to water the earth, because there were no people to cultivate the soil."

Dr. Monroe further states that God would not allow the plants to have the water they needed to grow because there were no people to man-age and control the growth. God held back the watering of the plants to prevent chaotic uncontrolled growth. He would not allow the environment to become chaotic because God is a God or order. Leadership and order must be in place before God blesses it with growth.

God's answer for creating order on earth was man. God created us and gave us dominion on earth to manage, rule, create order, govern, and put systems in place so that order is upheld. We are the environmental protection agency; we control earth's environment in accordance with the culture of heaven governing with the principles of God. In Genesis 1:26-27 God said, "Let us make man in our image, according to our likeness; let them have dominion over the fish of the sea, over the birds of the air, and over the cattle, over all the earth and over every creeping thing that creeps on the earth." So God created man in His own image; in the image of God He created him; male and female He created them.

We all have been commissioned and placed by God to use our gifts to rule the earth. And if the earth is in chaos, it means we are out of position and out of authority.

He gave it to us. Psalms 115:16 says, "The heavens are the LORD'S heavens, but the earth he has given to the children of mankind." God gave us this earth, the authority and principles to master it. Just like any corporation has a CEO, a president, and managers in every department, we too were all created to be man-agers in our department of gifting. We should operate business in accordance with the training and culture that were set by the head.

LIVING BENEATH OUR PRIVILEGE

"For the kingdom of God is not in word but in power."

[Dunamis power]

1 Corinthians 4:20

God gave us authority and power on earth to dominate and rule. The Bible Study Tools New Testament Lexicon defines dunamis power as strength, power, and ability. It further describes dunamis as "the power and influence which belong to riches and wealth," in the following sub categories:

A. Inherent power; power residing in a thing by virtue of its nature, or which a person or thing exerts or puts forth

B. Power for performing miracles

C. Moral power and excellence of soul

D. The power and influence which belong to riches and wealth

E. Power and resources arising from numbers

F. Power consisting in or resting upon armies, forces, hosts

The authority I am referring to is a Greek word called "exousia". Our authority gives us the authority to speak to any situation, pray for change, and be confident of our position as leaders because God gave us the exousia authority and placed us in position to dominate. We recognize our authority as believers in God but many believers tend to stop there. What we need to do is recognize and use our authority and power. 'Our power,' is another Greek word called "dunamis". Dunamis has close derivation to some common words we use like dynamite and dynamic. It is a word that does not just carry the meaning of having authority, but having the ability to assert the authority. It is an explosive and dynamic meaning which implies action and movement. In other words it is not just the ability to talk about change, it is the ability to make it happen. Dunamis is pronounced do-nam-is. Dunamis is when reasoning and talking is not working and it's time to explode into action and do something about it.

When I was a little boy my parents told me that I don't have to allow anyone to pick on me. I was issued the authority and power to exercise my right to freedom from being picked on by my peers. My mother told me I can stand in authority with my head held high never worrying about going to any neighborhood. But just in case someone infringed on my rights and decided to put their hands on me, my father taught me another power; And when my exousia authority didn't work, daddy's dunamis power would get the job done with a mean right hook to the jaw. Any bully foolish enough to ignore my exousia authority would have to deal with my dunamis power. Which would back up their understanding of my exousia and could result in rendering them under my feet, and I mean literally under my feet because they might get their head stomped. Dunamis power doesn't just walk in its authority, it demands and asserts it power. Dunamis is an action word and when authority is not respected, dunamis takes its respect.

We have authority to speak boldly, confidently just like Jesus did, knowing that we have been placed here by God as his mouthpieces, ambassadors and governing authority to dominate and rule the earth. We can assert that authority but there are those occasions where our authority is challenged and we need to assert our power in situations. Our power is in our money, our action, in working together, and in using our gifts and operating in God's purpose for our lives. We shouldn't just stop at praying for change, when we have the dunamis power to make change happen. We don't have to beg for cleaner more wholesome television programming when we have the dunamis power to own the television stations and make our own programs. We are gifted and powerful enough that when the world sees us using our gifts, they will go to great lengths to use our gifts. Our gifts and talent are our leverage for us to influence the world. We have the power as a group to band together and bring about the change that we were placed on earth to bring. We need never go to the world for a loan when God gave us the power to create wealth. We shouldn't have to pray for miracles in feeding the poor when God gave us the principles and power to feed the poor. We shouldn't be praying over situations we should be controlling. When the world doesn't respect our God given authority, Christians have the power to make them come under subjection to the will of God. When we are busy doing what God called us to do, we're not asking the world to change, we're creating that change.

God created earth and he placed us here for a specific reason. If we miss the reason for our existence then we have missed out on tremendous blessings and fulfillment for our lives. God put us on earth in a leadership position to control the earth based on the principles and culture of heaven.

He gave us the ability to create wealth, by using our gifts, and walking in our purpose in a specific job and by working with specific people to accomplish the goals he has set for our lives.

God never created earth to be a hostile, uncontrolled environment, full of evil and hardship. God created earth as a beautiful paradise for us to control and thrive in. The Garden of Eden was free from the corruption that we see in the world today. He gave us the authority and directions for maintaining the earth. We gave up control by deviating from his instructions but we still have access to his authority and principles. We don't have to sit on earth miserably waiting for Jesus to come back; we still have a purpose on earth and a mission to complete here. Earth is still a beautiful and delightful place that we can rule and enjoy.

Deuteronomy 8:18 says, God gave us the power to create wealth, but we seem to be content living in poverty.

Many of God's people have adopted a mindset that keeps them broke or living below the privileges that God has afforded them. So often Christians make declarations of their exousia authority but never exercise their dunamis power when it is needed most. We are like police officers that act like mall cops. We carry our badge but leave our gun at home.

We talk about the blessings of God but won't exercise the dunamis power to violently take what the devil stole from us. We pray but we don't have the wealth or political power to actually create change. We talk about doing God's work, but don't actually do it. The kingdom suffers violence, but the violent take it by force. (Matthew 11:12) We don't have to be walked over by the devil when we have a spiritual badge and a gun; we must use everything we got.

Often times we think of God in terms of a church building and religious practices instead of one who empowers us, gifts us, and sends us into the world to create change and impact the world with the culture of God. We miss our very reason for existence on earth and die without ever discovering what God placed inside of us when we don't exhaust our God given gifts, talents and abilities. Many people believe that God created them to do work in a church building when the church is not a building; we are the church or ekklesia; the Greek word used in the bible for church meaning called out to. (Bible study tools, 2016) Not called into a building every Sunday to sit in a pew for a few hours and have a place to be eulogized when you die. We are called out to go into the world and spread the culture of heaven creating good change and maintaining the earth the way God intended in the beginning of creation when he created the earth as a peaceful paradise. God's original intention for us on earth entitles us to blessings, management and prosperity because that was his original intention for us.

AVOIDANCE OF WEALTH

"And you shall remember the Lord your God, for it is He who gives you power to get wealth."

Deuteronomy 8:18

God created earth as a place of peace, provision, and abundance. The very mention of money produces a false and groundless guilt in many Christians; believing there is virtue in poverty. The worst part of our misunderstanding of the pursuit of wealth is that many of these beliefs are contrary to their biblical founding. That is, there are scriptures in the bible that have been misinterpreted concerning money that lead us to believe the acquisition of money and people with an abundance of money is evil. This belief is so far from being true. Let's look at a scripture in Matthew 19:16-22 NIV.

Jesus Counsels The Rich Young Ruler

Now behold, one came and said to Him, "Good Teacher, what good thing shall I do that I may have eternal life?" So He said to him, "Why do you call me good? No one is good but one, that is, God. But if you want to enter into life, keep the commandments." He said to Him, "Which ones?" Jesus said, "You shall not murder. You shall not commit adultery. You shall not steal. You shall not bear false witness. Honor your father and your mother, and you shall love your neighbor as yourself." The young man said to Him, "All these things I have kept from my youth. What do I still lack?" Jesus said to him, "If you want to be perfect, go, sell what you have and give to the poor, and you will have treasure in heaven; and come, follow Me." But when the young man heard that saying, he went away sorrowful, for he had great possessions.

Jesus informs us that with God all things are possible. In verse 23 Jesus said to His disciples, "Assuredly, I say to you that it is hard for a rich man to enter the kingdom of heaven. And again I say to you, it is easier for a camel to go through the eye of a needle than for a rich man to enter the kingdom of God."

When His disciples heard this, they were greatly astonished, saying in verse 24, "Who then can be saved?" But Jesus looked at them and said, "With men this is impossible, but with God all things are possible."

Everyone who reads this pericope quickly presumes that Jesus is condemning the acquisition of wealth and the wealthy; not true. Throughout scripture God blesses His people with overwhelming wealth and riches; Job, Abraham, Isaac, Jacob, David, Joseph, all great men of God who were filthy rich and went to heaven. This interaction between Jesus and the rich man would lead us to believe that it was the wealth that had this man heading to hell. At the end of this interaction between Jesus and the rich man even the disciples were fearful because their understanding of this conversation between Jesus and this man was misunderstood. After carefully dissecting the context of this scripture, the historical context, the underlying messages, and the true purpose behind this conversation you will come to a very different conclusion concerning this verse.

In the first line of text the man approaches Jesus and calls him good teacher. This was a common greeting used in greeting a teacher or rabbi in these days which implies that the man is intrinsically good or that he could be good enough "in works" to get himself into heaven. At this time the Jewish people believed they were saved by works alone. They had many rituals and traditions they would adhere to and their adherence to these traditions were believed to be sufficient for saving their souls.

Jesus came to disprove this and to die for us because we can only be saved by Gods grace not works. The belief that you can save yourself leads to boastfulness, pride, arrogance, self righteousness, and condescension of others who are less fortunate than yourself.

> "For by grace you have been saved through faith, and that not of yourselves; it is the gift of God, not of works, lest anyone should boast." (Ephesians 2:8-9)

Jesus came against the belief of men being good based on their works because there was a lot of boasting and pride associated with the statement good teacher. Many were prideful and condescending because they did not realize how sinful they were. The first thing Jesus corrected was that no man is good. Even though Jesus was good because He was God, He understood that this man did not know He was God. When he asked the rhetorical question, "Why do you call me good?" You don't know I'm God, so "why do you call me good?" Jesus corrects him by saying no man is good.

The man, still gloating and prideful in verse 16 goes on to ask the rhetorical question, "What do I need to do to receive eternal life?"

The question is rhetorical because this man is very confident that he has already met the requirements for eternal life. He was very wealthy, educated, and he was raised under the laws all his life; he knew what he needed to do according to the Jewish law. But he wanted to gloat in his accomplishments. His whole purpose of coming to Jesus was to boast about himself. Jesus knowing his true intention plays into his hand by giving him the expected Jewish response in verses 18 and 19 about keeping the commandments. The man bubbling over in pride finally gets the opportunity to gloat when in verse 20 he says, "I have kept these from my youth." In other words the young man is saying, I'm perfect because I have always kept these since I was a boy. In asking the question to Jesus of "What else can I do?" He expected Jesus to say, 'You're good, keep doing what you're doing and you're guaranteed to get into heaven.' Instead Jesus exposed the truth in that he is not as perfect as he thought he was.

". . . for it is He who gives you power to get wealth."

Deuteronomy 8:18

Jesus knew he was prideful and that he was not as sold out in his devotion for God as he thought so he tells him to do something he knows he is unwilling to do; give up his wealth. The man is unwilling to give up his wealth and is convicted of his love of money over his love of God. He violated the

Jewish law or obligation of Tzedakah which is charity for the less fortunate. An old Jewish adage is, "Your only as wealthy as what you are willing to give away."

Despite negative stereotypes, the Jewish people were and still are some of the most generous and philanthropic cultures and people of faith. Despite the fact that Jews are close to approximately 2% of the United States population their dollar amount of charitable giving ranks up in the top percentages of giving by American ethnic groups. Charitable giving is built right into Jewish culture; laws governing generosity especially to the poor are ranked high in Jewish faith. The Jewish Talmud states that you are only as wealthy as the amount you are willing to give away. In Leviticus it is forbidden for farmers to reap the whole harvest of their land because something must be left for the poor and less fortunate to gather and eat from.

In the passage, the young man goes away with his head held down in a posture of humility at the exposing of his sinfulness in being unwilling to give to the poor. His pride and arrogance kept him from coming to a place of repentance. This scripture has nothing to do with the virtues of poverty but pride coming to humility and the sinfulness of all men.

Pride is dangerous because pride puts you in a mindset of already having attained perfection. We must be humble as we approach God because as long as you are prideful and think you are perfect, God cannot correct you. You can't improve on perfection and you'll never repent if you feel there is no need for repentance. You can't bring redemption to someone who stubbornly believes redemption is unnecessary. James 4:6 says, "God opposes the proud, but gives grace to the humble."

The young man's wealth hindered him because his belief at this time was that if God blesses us with wealth then the true evidence of Godliness is wealth; and the more wealth you have, the more God you have. We know that this is not true because God has always been a God of the poor as he asked the man to sell all he has for the poor. He had to be humbled to understand that in spite of his wealth his heart was still sinful. Through challenging his willingness to give up his wealth for the work of God, God exposes the truly sinful condition of his heart. He loved wealth more than he loved God.

Money Is Essential For Everyone

To overlook money with a false humility and an overemphasized persona is an unbiblical approach toward how God views money. Money gives us the benefits of doing an abundance of good work. God would not forbid us from acquiring wealth; God encourages building wealth. God blessed his beloved people in the Old Testament with ridiculous wealth and even in the New Testament. He gives instructions to wealthy people for doing his work. In fact God has instructions for the rich of this world in 1 Timothy 6:17-19.

Instructions To The Rich

"Command those who are rich in this present age not to be haughty, nor to trust in uncertain riches but in the living God, who gives us richly all things to enjoy. Let them do good, that they be rich in good works, ready to give, willing to share, storing up for themselves a good foundation for the time to come, that they may lay hold on eternal life."

"... for it is He who gives you power to get wealth."

Deuteronomy 8:18

Money Serves An Essential Purpose In God's Plan

Money matters because like every other institution on earth it serves a huge purpose as long as it is used with a Godly perspective. Drugs are only bad if they are abused. For example, Heroin is bad when taken in a back alley by someone who is only looking for a quick thrill. However, the correct dosage of the same drug after a painful operation can be essential for a comfortable and successful recovery. In fact, no hospital will operate without an abundant inventory of drugs. Drugs are a common and essential ingredient for any and every serious recuperation and we are successful in using them year after year with millions of patients because they are being used appropriately in the purpose they were created to be used in.

It would be foolish for us to ban drugs from a hospital or to avoid talking about the use of drugs by people who need them for recovery. It is just as foolish for Christians to avoid talking about money. We as Christians are the world's hospital that no longer allows the discussion of an essential element to the healing of the world's ailments; drug use. Every hospital has a fully stocked drug inventory with more than enough. They are always interacting with pharmaceutical companies to make sure they never run out. God's people have taken a taboo approach to the acquisition of money. We have forfeited our full potential because of the lack of it and we are deceived into believing that God is alright with us not having it when He requires us to be good stewards of it, invest it, grow it, and have dominion; and the proper and responsible use of it. God's work is not being done because we have been negligent in the area of finances. Money is essential for ministry; the more money we have, the more ministries we can handle. As long as we are financially strapped in a financially progressive world, we will struggle to progress in doing God's work. How can we take care of our families without money? Where will we live without money? How do we reach out to other countries and help the poor if we are the poor? As a body, we teach with inferior educational knowledge because we can't afford good education. Ultimately then, we suffer greater temptations because desperate people tend to be tempted to do desperate things. In the end it is God's purpose that is not working through us because we don't have the financial means to carry his work out. The world listens to economic power but we have no voice because we lack the economy. It's no wonder that the people that God created to control and dominate the earth with the culture of God, have become a non-factor; the continued decline of our society is partly due to the decline of our ability to influence financially.

Money is essential for ministry and it is a trick of the enemy for God's people to believe that we should be financially lacking. God wants us to have as much wealth as we can handle without loving his wealth more than we love him. It is for this reason only that everyone will not be wealthy because everyone can't handle great wealth. Money is not the root of all evil but the love of money is the root of all evil and when we love money more than we love God, evil is soon to take over.

It was God who gave us the power to create wealth. "And you shall remember the Lord your God, for it is He who gives you power to get wealth."

Deuteronomy 8:18

We have the power and knowledge to build businesses and create jobs. We have everything we need to be a dominant financial power on earth but we must tear down the old taboos of money and realize that there is no virtue in poverty. We need to have an abundance of money to help resolve the abundance of problems in the world today.

God never meant for us to avoid wealth or live beneath our rights as heirs to his kingdom. It's crazy to believe that God wants us to struggle financially and not have money enough to take care of our families and help the poor. Why would God create the institutions of business and wealth and his own heirs not be the benefactors of them? Is it reasonable to say that God left great wealth on earth for evil men to use for evil things while he gave dominion on earth to his children but expects them to remain broke, discouraged, and left to beg from the evil one? No! God gave us dominion on earth, wealth, businesses, power, gifts and influence to do good things on earth. We are here to be good stewards over the earth and carry the culture of heaven. God simply wants us to have the right perspective on money. God doesn't want us to develop a love of money more than we love him who gives us the power to create wealth.

MONEY IS A RESOURCE FOR CONVEYING WHAT'S IN YOUR YOUR HEART

"A good person produces good things from the treasure of a good heart, and an evil person produces evil things from the treasure of an evil heart."

Luke 6:45

You can tell what a person loves by where they spend their time and money. Jesus said, "Where your treasure is, there your heart will be also." (Matthew 6:21) Jesus is simply saying you spend your money on what you love. Jesus went on to say in Luke 6:45, "A good person produces good things from the treasury of a good heart, and an evil person produces evil things from the treasury of an evil heart." Money is one of our greatest resources. The bible says in Ecclesiastes 10:19 that money answers all things and the more money you have, the more answers you can provide. Whatever is in your heart money is a means to acquire it. What you acquire is a reflection of what's in your heart because money is a resource to convey what is in your heart. I love my family, so I'll spend my time and a whole lot of money going out to eat with my family. I'll spare no expense on a great vacation for my family. I love God so I have never had a problem with being very generous in tithing to my church. If your heart desires evil things, money will make it possible to carry it out. If someone loves women, it does not matter how ugly they are, money will make women available to them. If you love drugs, money will make drugs available to you. If you love cars, as long as you have the money to buy them, you will have cars of all kinds lined up in your garages. Whatever is in you, will be brought to fruition with an abundance of money.

The drug cartels have free reign in the country of Mexico because they have more money than the government (Park, 2016). The government has absolutely no control over them because they are the dominant economic power. The cartels have money to bribe the police officers and the police will accept the bribes because their checks are barely enough to take care of their families. When the police try to raid drug cartels, the cartels have better overwhelming firepower. The cartels have more personnel with better military training. The cartels control the media and make movies to promote cartel lifestyles. They can portray cartel lifestyle as a good and glamorous career in order to attract more recruits and garner the support of the citizens. If the cartels commit a murder, they just bribe or kill all the detectives which is why most murders in Mexico never get prosecuted. The country suffers violence because the hearts of the people ruling it are violent and the money is a means for asserting the will of the evil in their hearts. When evil people have more money then the good people; the good will suffer and the evil will flourish.

Pablo Escobar was a dominant financial power in Columbia (Minster, 2016). He was a dominant political power, he was able to change government policies and avoid arrest by killing politicians and blowing up government buildings. He had so much power and influence that he convinced the government to give him a very short prison term which he spent in a plush and extravagant prison that he built with his money. He hired the guards and had everything his heart desired brought to him, prostitutes, gourmet meals and famous soccer players. His heart was corrupt and he had the financial means to convey his will from the corruption in his heart. And the country was corrupt because the financial power was corrupt.

All through history you can see dominant financial powers imposing their will on societies. Our country was founded on Christian beliefs as one country under God because Christians were the dominant financial power and thereby held the greatest influence. It may have been a pseudo Christianity and by no means am I implying that we were morally perfect or even true to our Christian beliefs as a country however, if you compare us to a country like Germany in 1944 when they were in the process of taking over the world and exterminating all non-whites and Jews, I'm glad that financially we had a leg up on them. It is because of our financial backing that we were able to produce the nuclear

"A good person produces good things from the treasury of a good heart, . . ."

Luke 6:45

bomb before the Germans and Japanese during World War 2. More money helped us develop well trained soldiers with better weapons. Our show of force looks different than the German's show of force because we were founded on justice and the Germans were founded on hate. There were rules of engagement; we tried to aid citizens on all sides who were displaced. Drug cartels and Nazi fanatics used no discretion, rules of engagement, and had no consciences about murdering innocent men, women, and children. What they had in their heart was racial hatred and the selfish ambition of world domination and absolute power. Their money provided the means for conveying what was in their heart.

Even now as Russia is trying to assert dominance over its neighboring country Ukraine, the first step America and its allies took against deterring their behavior was economic sanctions (Ukraine Today, 2016). We begin to restrict their ability to make money. The less money they have, the less havoc they can wreak. We won't trade or buy goods from them, we stop loaning money to them, because if we can cut off their economic power, they are impotent and unable to assert their will and dominance in any region.

Terrorists are strong not because they are fanatics, not because of their dedication and hard work, not because they pray a lot, but they have billions of dollars in oil money and they have the means to carry out their agenda. Terrorism would stop in one day if we had the ability to stop their cash flow. When we get rid of cash, and everyone's cash is registered into a global data base and currency is only exchanged from a mark on the hand or the forehead, then nuclear weapons and any other terrorist device cannot be purchased without scanning the hand or forehead and there is always a record of exchange because every transaction goes through the global database. It's a great concept that's going to end badly because the Antichrist will provide the solution and many will accept the solution out of desperation. Money is at the root of it and money is only evil if the hearts of the people using it are evil.

The Jewish community is able to affect the American government to the point where any attack on the mother country of Israel is seen as an attack on America because Jewish Americans have such a dominant financial and political power in the United States that they are able to impose their will in government policy. Roland Martin cited a figure that the Jewish dollar stays in the Jewish community 19 days and the Jewish community is supportive of each other as a race.

What about Christians? Within the Christian church, you can typically find churches trying to do things just to keep the lights on; we can't even begin to go out into every nation to save souls. We have racial agendas and political agendas but we forget that we are here for God's agenda. God gave Christians the principles for building wealth through working, building businesses, and tithing. The very people that God gave the principles for wealth to, neglect to use them. The world system uses the biblical principles we should be using and they are using dominion that was originally intended for us to impose their will on earth. The reason the earth suffers evil and corruption is because the hearts of the people with the money are corrupt. Christians are dedicated, loyal to God, willing to evangelize and help, but when it's time to execute and actually do God's good work on earth, we don't have the money to pull it off. After any natural disaster in Haiti or a tsunami in Thailand the world is outraged at the calamities and want to help. Secular Movie actors will donate millions of dollars, secular music artist will donate millions of dollars, secular corporations will donate millions of dollars and most of the Christians will just pray because we don't have any money. It is outrageous that the very people who were given (by Almighty God) the authority over the world systems

"A good person produces good things from the treasury of a good heart, . . ."

Luke 6:45

of finance, medicine etc., and the principals in the word of God to develop and acquire mastery of them, are lacking in them more than the secular world. We should be the dominant power on earth so that every drug cartel that rises up is crushed and kneeling at the feet of God. Every terrorist organization is dismantled and kneeling at the feet of God and every country that tries to overthrow its neighboring countries is rendered impotent and is forced to submit to the will and authority of God and his people.

But if you desire the things of God in your heart you will see that reflected in the lives of the people of God. Churches with sincere hearts and the money to do ministry help millions of people. They reach out to other countries, they buy homes for elderly members who can't afford to stay anywhere. They spare no expense in hiring musicians and creating a worship experience for God because their love of God is conveyed to God in their worship. And without the impediment of a lack of money, God's ministry is uninhibited. And with the abundance of money and an abundance of love for the things of God, this entire world can be changed. Many of the people of God have always spent time working in the ministry but they lack the money to bring ministry visions to fruition. If the people of God used God's biblical principles to acquire wealth and out of the abundance of love in their heart tithed and gave to the work of the Lord, world hunger would be completely eradicated. Christians with money can control the world, creation of laws, politics, all forms of media, evil dictatorships would be overthrown and almost the entire known world would give their lives to Christ.

Money is a means for carrying out what's in your heart. Proverbs 22:7 says, "The rich rule over the poor, and the borrower is servant to the lender." If the world system is evil, it's because the people with the money are evil. If we are being ruled over by evil people, it's because we are the poor and the rich are evil. The people with the wealth have the ability to rule and impose the will of their hearts. But when God's people have all the money, the world systems should be pure, righteous, and holy; but it's only holy if God's people are holy. Our hearts must be prepared and made ready to receive and carry out good things with the wealth that God gives.

GOD GIVES FINANCIAL PROVISION FOR HIS VISION

"And God will generously provide all you need. Then you will always have everything you need and plenty left over to share with others."

2 Corinthians 9:8

God gives us provision for his vision. God's money is not necessarily just for us, but it is for us to carry out his good work. Our lives are not about us because we were created for a specific purpose. God makes it very clear in scripture that he doesn't have a hang up about giving us more than enough money, in fact he wants his people to have as much money as they can possibly handle according to the following scriptures:

2 Corinthians 9:8 says, "And God will generously provide

all you need. Then you will always have everything you need and plenty left over to share with others."

Matthew 6:33 says, "But seek first the kingdom of God and His righteousness, and all these things shall be added to you."

Proverbs 3:9-10 says, "Honor the Lord with your possessions, and with the first fruits of all your increase; so your barns will be filled with plenty, and your vats will overflow with new wine."

Philippians 4:19 says, "And my God shall supply all your needs according to His riches in glory by Christ Jesus."

Malachi 3:10-11 says, "Bring all the tithes into the storehouse, that there may be food in My house, and try Me now in this," says the Lord of hosts. "If I will not open for you the windows of heaven and pour out for you such blessing that there will not be room enough to receive it. And I will rebuke the devourer for your sakes, so that he will not destroy the fruit of your ground, nor shall the vine fail to bear fruit for you in the field," says the Lord of hosts.

We must be prepared to receive what God gives us. If God is so generous in giving out financial blessings, why aren't all his people wealthy? Why did Jesus say, "The poor you will have with you always." (Matthew 26:11) There are many reasons why there will always be poor among us; some of which are no fault of the individual, but I have found that most people sabotage their own financial success by being out of the will of God. Many people mishandle the money they get. Some seek to get rich for the wrong reasons, some open businesses with no other motive than just making money. If God's purpose is not behind your drive then don't expect him to drive your success. God has given us everything we need for success; access to His abundant provision to carry out His purpose in our lives. God is fine with us prospering as His work is prospering however many pursue God's prosperity and neglect pursuing Him. They seek to manipulate God only to obtain things.

Not everyone will own a business or amass great wealth but if all God's people are in position, no one will lack. Even the poor will receive more than enough when the wealthy people of God have a generous heart. In God's plan, out of the abundance of wealth, God gives provision for his work through us. He gives us the money to do his business and we keep the change. The bible says in, James 4:2-3 "You lust and do not have. You murder and covet and cannot obtain. You fight and war. Yet you do not have because you do not ask. You ask and do not receive, because you ask amiss, that you may spend it on your pleasures."

Our selfishness does not move God to provide provision. God is not concerned with us using him to accomplish our purpose of chasing worldly desires, but God wants us to follow after his purposes. God loans us his money while we're on earth to carry out his purposes in our lives and to take care of us. We are his investment but before God blesses us with wealth, there are some prerequisites that must be met.

If you were going to obtain an automobile loan to purchase a vehicle, the bank won't give you money and take your word that you're going to do what you said you were going to do with the money. There are prerequisites that must be determined before they give you money for the car. No good investor invests in anything unless they think it is a worthwhile investment. They want to make sure that the money they are lending is going to increase its value; they won't allow you to purchase a vehicle with high mileage because the high mileage vehicles are less valuable and susceptible to breakdowns. People don't pay car notes on broken down cars. You can't drive a broken down car to work. There is no return on investment from something that is not working or producing anything profitable. There is a process that the bank goes through to make sure you're committed to using it for its purpose, and being able to pay it back.

God works the same way. God puts us through a process to make sure we are committed to his purpose. He doesn't just give money but we must go through a process. Are we paying tithes because we love him and are called according to his purpose or are we tithing because some false prophet portrayed God as a cosmic slot machine that we can give money to and make some quick easy magic money? The bible talks about false teachers who use corrupt teaching methods to manipulate people into giving their money to them.

1 Timothy 6:5 speaks about the useless wrangling of men of corrupt minds who are destitute of the truth, and suppose that godliness is a means of gain. From such withdraw yourself.

Titus 1:10-11 speaks of the Elder's task. "For there are many insubordinate, both idle talkers and deceivers, especially those of the circumcision, whose mouths must be stopped, who subvert whole households, teaching things which they ought not for the sake of dishonest gain." God doesn't want us more in love with his money than we are with him. Money can corrupt good people so he must screen us and test us. He tells us in 1 Timothy 6:6, "Now godliness with contentment is great gain."

We must set our focus on God so that we are not pulled into the deceitful corruptions of money. God puts us through a process of testing to be sure that we're strong enough to handle his money and be good stewards of it.

Luke 16:10-12 says, "He who is faithful in what is least is faithful also in much; and he who is unjust in what is least is unjust also in much. Therefore if you have not been faithful in the unrighteous mammon, who will commit to your trust the true riches? And if you have not been faithful in what is another man's, who will give you what is your own?"

God may leave you in a period of financial trouble sometimes to see if you are committed and faithful in being a good steward over the little that you have before rewarding you with a lot. There is a testing period to determine if God is in your heart so that when he gives you money, his purpose will be conveyed with it.

PREPARED FOR WEALTH

"Heal the sick, cleanse the lepers, and raise the dead, cast out demons. Freely you have received, freely give. Provide neither gold nor silver nor copper in your money belts, nor bag for your journey, nor two tunics, nor sandals, nor staffs; for a worker is worthy of his food."

Matthew 10:8-10

In Matthew 10:1 Jesus speaks to the twelve apostles. "And when He had called His twelve disciples to Him, He gave them power over unclean spirits, to cast them out, and to heal all kinds of sickness and all kinds of disease."

Jesus gave His disciples the power to go out and perform miracles with the intent of bringing people to change their hearts and come to Christ. The working of miracles was just an experience that was designed to attract the people and show the realities of the true power of God on earth. God is really after their souls.

Jesus gave the disciples these gifts and he gave them very specific instructions on carrying out their duties as newly appointed leaders.

In Matthew 10:8-10 Jesus says, "Heal the sick, cleanse the lepers, and raise the dead, cast out demons. Freely you have received, freely give. Provide neither gold nor silver nor copper in your money belts, nor bag for your journey, nor two tunics, nor sandals, nor staffs; for a worker is worthy of his food."

Jesus first lets them know that he has given them these gifts free of charge so they are not to use these gifts selfishly of just for the purposes of making money. Jesus knew that the disciples were going to encounter a lot of people and there would be lots of money involved. People would be willing to pay anything in their time of desperation to be rid of a demon or to heal a dying loved one but Jesus wanted to teach them that their focus was Christ. We are not looking to take but to give.

At the same time He tells them not to take money with them because the people have a responsibility to take care of them. What is the lesson we are to learn from Jesus' instructions? The lesson is in our obligation to do the work of the Lord whether we are compensated or not. The people have an obligation to take care of those that take care of them. In the same way we can't expect vegetables to grow from the ground if we don't dig around them and fertilize them we must make sure we take care of the people who intercede for our souls so that their interceding is not hindered by their natural needs.

Money has distracting properties and if the focus is placed on money, the purity of the gospel will be tarnished and we will worship the created money rather than the God of the blessings. They had to learn discipline and the importance of the focus before they were told to go out for the express purpose of gathering and making money. After they had been matured as leaders they were able to handle money.

We have to be disciplined in understanding our focus before God blesses us with handling the acquisition of money because he said seek ye first the kingdom of heaven and all these things (money) shall be added unto you. We can prosper as a result of the use of our gifts but the purpose of our gifts and time on earth is to do the will of God.

USING WHAT WE HAVE TO PRODUCE WEALTH

"We all possess something of the highest rarity that can never be recovered or replicated…"

Don't miss your value. If we are going to use our gifts to produce wealth, the first thing we must do is understand the value behind what we have. There is a very rare metal called platinum. We know what platinum is and the tremendous value that it holds. If I were to try and trade a gold ring for a platinum ring, you wouldn't accept that trade because you understand that platinum is rarer than gold; hence it is more valuable. Our understanding of the metal causes us to value it, protect it, and use it to our benefit.

In the 16th century you couldn't give it away because when the

Spanish first encountered it in Ecuador they thought it was gold that had not fully cured. People used it to make counterfeit gold coins and the problem got so bad that the Spanish and English governments gathered up all the platinum in the country and dumped it into the ocean. Little did they know that they were trying to pass off a more valuable product for a much lesser product. It was only because they didn't understand the value of the product and as a result they threw away billions of dollars that was sitting right in their house. (Don Gumber, 2013)

In my observation, too many people walk around every day broke, impoverished and discouraged trying to find a way out of their financial rut. Many people try to pass themselves off as someone they are not in an attempt to make money. What they don't realize is that they are trying to be someone or something that is lesser value than who they are. If they knew the value of who they were, they would invest in themselves instead of trying to be someone else.

God made us infinitely unique and wonderful. He said we are all fearfully and wonderfully made but if we never acknowledge who we are in Christ and the value in the uniqueness he placed in us, we will never properly invest in ourselves. Like the Spanish, we'll throw our gifts into the bottom of an ocean of obscurity and the world will never get the opportunity to enjoy the gift to the world that we are. So the next time someone says,"Who do you think you are; God's gift to the world?" You can confidently say, "Yes I am!"

It is important that we recognize the value of who we are and stay preoccupied in doing what we are called to do. We cannot be idle looking around at what others are doing or we can become jealous of what they're doing because we haven't applied ourselves to what we should be doing. We'll hate them for knowing their value because we don't know ours or we try to become a cheap imitation of them when we could have been a dynamic original if we only knew what we possessed.

We all possess something of the highest rarity that can never be recovered or replicated once it's gone. Our part in working with others and using our gift(s) is so important because of the irreplace-ability of our position on earth. No one can be you better than you and once you realize how uniquely valuable you are, you can see yourself as the great person God created you to be.

There is a connection between the rarity of our gift and large returns. How do we make money using our gifts? What is the science behind building wealth? I was talking to a woman who worked at a fast food chain store and she was talking to a gentleman who was an electrician.

He was discussing how much money he made and how easy his job was. The woman who worked at the restaurant worked extremely hard and didn't make manager; even after working there for 6 years. She was one of the hardest working employees I had ever seen and she told the electrician, I should make more money than you because I work twice as hard as you. Too many people think this logic makes sense. We are told that if you work hard, you'll do well in life. The harder we work, the more money we should make. The reality of the situation is that you don't make more money based on how hard you work. Your pay is based on your value to the client. The more people the client can find to do your job, the less money you will be paid to do it. The less people the client can find to do your job, the more money you can demand for the job.

If I were a nuclear physicist and I was the only person in the world who knew how to disarm a nuclear bomb and a nuclear bomb was about to go off, I could demand a trillion dollars to disarm the bomb because no one else in the world has the ability to do what I know how to do. It doesn't matter if the job takes me 5 seconds to disarm it; I'll make a trillion dollars in five seconds flat. It doesn't matter if all I do is press one button to disarm it; I'll make a trillion dollars by pressing one button because I have a rare and unique ability that can only be achieved by me.

Movie actors get paid millions of dollars just to play an easy role in a film because they fit the role perfectly. It doesn't matter how easy the job is because the uniqueness of their gift makes them invaluable to the success of the film.

We all have a unique gift but if we never use it then we will miss the opportunity to produce wealth during our lifetime. Therefore we must discover the areas that we are talented and uniquely gifted in. Then we can perfect it and market it to produce wealth; there's money in your gifts and talents.

TAKING RISKS

"Without faith it's impossible to please God."

Hebrew 11:6

We must take risks and invest in what God gives us. Jesus spoke about three men who were given talents. The talents are representative of whatever we have, money, gifts etc. In this parable Jesus brings out some points about how we should handle what he has given us.

Matthew 25:14-30 Teaches on the Parable of the Talents:

"For the kingdom of heaven is like a man traveling to a far country, who called his own servants and delivered his goods to them. And to one he gave five talents, to another two, and to another one, to each according to his own ability; and immediately he went on a journey.

Then he who had received the five talents went and

traded with them, and made another five talents. And likewise he who had received two gained two more also. But he who had received one went and dug in the ground, and hid his lord's money. After a long time the lord of those servants came and settled accounts with them.

So he who had received five talents came and brought five other talents, saying, 'Lord, you delivered to me five talents; look, I have gained five more talents besides them.' His lord said to him, 'Well done, good and faithful servant; you were faithful over a few things, I will make you ruler over many things. Enter into the joy of your lord.' He also who had received two talents came and said, 'Lord, you delivered to me two talents; look, I have gained two more talents besides them.' His lord said to him, 'Well done, good and faithful servant; you have been faithful over a few things, I will make you ruler over many things. Enter into the joy of your lord.'

Then he who had received the one talent came and said, 'Lord, I knew you to be a hard man, reaping where you have not sown, and gathering where you have not scattered seed. And I was afraid, and went and hid your talent in the ground. Look, there you have what is yours.'

But his lord answered and said to him, 'You wicked and lazy servant, you knew that I reap where I have not sown, and gather where I have not scattered seed. So you ought to have deposited my money with the bankers, and at my coming I would have received back my own with interest. So take the talent from him, and give it to him who has ten talents.

For to everyone who has, more will be given, and he will have abundance; but from him who does not have, even what he has will be taken away. And cast the unprofitable servant into the outer darkness. There will be weeping and gnashing of teeth.'"

God requires us to take risks in investing and being aggressive in seeking a return on that investment. I was always taught to get a job and to stay away from starting a business. Place your money in low risk bank accounts that give meager returns on investment but have the least amount of risk for a loss. I believed a career as a musician was too unstable; and investing in college after a certain age is too risky. "Don't become an artist! Have you ever heard of starving artists?" You're not guaranteed a job in the musical theater or in music or any unconventional job, but what if you are gifted in these areas? What if you're calling and gift in life is unconventional? How do you know if you will become the wealthiest or most successful artist unless you invest in yourself and try? Choosing more practical vocations is the path most of us choose and sometimes we miss the gift that is in us because it's not practical. Pursuing anything great carries risk and if you're not willing to take the risk, the scriptures imply that maybe you're not worthy of the reward.

This scripture goes against everything I have ever known about how we should handle money and invest in ourselves. Maybe creating a low risk stable environment is not always the thing we should do.

During the time that this parable was written there were no banks to put their talents or money in. They had to make long arduous trips along dangerous roads where thieves and robbers could rob and murder them. It was a huge risk just leaving the safety of where they were. It was much safer to dig a hole and bury what they had. At least it wouldn't get stolen. The two wise men took a tremendous risk going after the return on investment by traveling to town where they could invest. The fool did the more practical and safer thing by burying his talent in a hole where it was safe from thieves. It was the safest thing to do; he wouldn't lose money, but he wouldn't gain anything either. According to how most people live we would have buried what we had also. The wise men received a reward because they invested. They took a calculated risk and brought back a return. Even if they lost something at least they tried. We have to have faith enough to at least try in life. If you take a risk you might win, but if you never even try you'll fail before you start.

What Jesus is saying in this parable is that God wants us to have faith and be courageous. "Without faith it's impossible to please God." (Hebrew 11:6) The evidence of courage is the presence of fear. If you are not afraid you cannot be courageous. Courage is when you are afraid but you must persevere in spite of your fear. God never called us to do small safe things because you don't need him to do small things. God wants to do great and big things in your life, and if you are not intimidated by the magnitude of the vision that God gives you then it probably didn't come from God. God always calls us to do great things that seem overwhelming to us. Moses was intimidated by what God commissioned him to do, King David was intimidated at times, but God was glorified because they could have never accomplishments what they did without God.

How many of us never start the businesses that God placed in our heart to start because the safe thing to do is to work a job? How many people die and never use the gifts God gave them? How many people never go to school to invest in the vocation or talents God blessed them with? (culinary arts, comedy, writing, business, theater, music, personal training and fitness) We forego the areas we are gifted in for areas that we have a more stable opportunity in. God wants us to have faith in him and invest in the gifts he gave us. Sometimes we must be responsible and keep our jobs in order to take care of our families but we should be working towards investing and going after the greater return so that when the time is right, we can take advantage of the opportunity. Never be irresponsible with your family but get out of the mindset of never taking risks. Sometimes we do what we have to do until we can do what we're called to do. We must be working and investing in our gifts so that in God's kairos timing we are able to go after the opportunities that God presents to us.

WE HAVE TO UNDERSTAND THE DANGERS OF MONEY

"But those who desire to be rich fall into temptation and a snare, and into many foolish and harmful lusts which drown men in destruction and perdition."

1 Timothy 6:9

God promised us wealth in his word. 2 Corinthians 9:8 says, "And God is able to make all grace abound toward you, that you, always having all sufficiency in all things, may have an abundance for every good work."

Philippians 4:19 says, "And my God shall supply all your needs according to His riches in glory by Christ Jesus."

God backs up his people and provides more than enough for his ministry and our needs, and if money is a resource for conveying what's in your heart, God must make sure we have the right heart or the money he gives us will be used for evil. God gives money to people he can trust it with. God won't give you anything that will cause you to turn away from him. Lots of money can corrupt the best people so it is important to have a pure heart. Job had a good heart and a fierce resolve to hold on to his integrity. This is why God was able to bless him with a ridiculous amount of wealth. Job was filthy rich and because his heart was pure, his riches didn't corrupt him.

Can you handle the wealth? We want money but the question is, 'Are we able to handle the money we ask for?' The bible describes the dangers of money given to the wrong people or given too soon before the heart is prepared for the abundance.

1 Timothy 6:9 says, "But those who desire to be rich fall into temptation and a snare, and into many foolish and harmful lusts which drown men in destruction and perdition."

We can easily lose ourselves in the temptations that come with money. I've seen Christians who have come off of drugs and God blessed them with great high paying jobs. They paid off all their bills, and had excess money sitting in their bank accounts. With plenty of money to spend, their minds went back to what they used to love; drugs. As a result they went back to using drugs. Some of us love the Lord when we're broke; we're singing, 'I'm in love with Jesus,' but as soon as we get some money we're singing, 'I'm in love with the Coco.' Why would God give us anything that is going to turn us away from him? God wants you closer to Him; he won't give you anything to turn you away from him. If money brought you closer to him, he would continue to increase your finances, but if it causes you to turn away from him he'll hold it back from you until you're ready to handle it. God doesn't want to withhold anything good from you any more than you would want to withhold good things from your own children and loved ones, but if the gift is going to hurt you it must be withheld.

Any responsible parent that has a child that is of driving age will consider if their child is responsible enough to drive before buying a car for their child. A car can be a huge blessing to take their siblings to their appointments, drive to an after school job, or they can use it to start a business and become a teen-preneur. But if they are not ready for it, it must be withheld.

The love of money is the root of all evil. The love of money is centered on selfishness, money for selfish desires, so if you love money more than God, you will take the money he gave you to use for his purposes and spend it on your own selfish desires. We've all mis-allocated and misappropriated funds. But if we want to experience great wealth we must be able to handle great responsibility because to whom much is given, much will be required of them. The more money God gives us, the more work He'll expect done. With more money, more poor people can be clothed, fed, and housed. More ministries must have more than enough money to operate.

What God does is he prepares your heart. God will allow you to have as much money as you can handle without turning away from him. Psalms 37:4 says, "Delight yourself also in the Lord; and He shall give you the desires of your heart." Not only will God give you your desires but through delighting in him through relationship with him, he will give you a better understanding of his word and he will also develop new desires in you. He will put desires in your heart that align with his vision. God gives you the heart that he wants you to have in order to convey his message of love to the world in you're giving and he also makes financial provision for you to carry it out.

Psalms 84:11 says, "For the Lord God is a sun and shield; The Lord will give grace and glory; No good thing will He withhold from those who walk uprightly."

Stay in relationship with God. Allow God to purify your heart. Be willing to submit to the will and direction of God and watch God blow your mind with the blessings he has in store for you. Remember in Luke 6:45 Jesus said, "A good man out of the good treasure of his heart brings forth good; and an evil man out of the evil treasure of his heart brings forth evil." And when God sees that you have a good heart, he knows you are a wise place to invest his money.

ENVIRONMENTAL PROTECTION AGENCY

"Let any one of you who is without sin be the first to throw a stone at her. Again he stooped down and wrote on the ground. At this, those who heard began to go away one at a time, the older ones first, until only Jesus was left with the woman still standing there. Jesus straightened up and asked her, "Woman, where are they? Has no one condemned you?" "No one, sir," she said. "Then neither do I condemn you," Jesus declared. "Go now and leave your life of sin."

John 8:7-11

In the beginning in the Garden of Eden; where God originally intended us to live and thrive, the Lord created us. Before He created us,

God created an environment conducive to the sustaining of our human lives and well being. He called that place Eden. God had to create an environment that was conducive to the needs of mankind before he placed mankind in the garden because if he hadn't, we could not survive. We need oxygen to breathe, and land to live on so God created the heavens (sky and atmosphere) and the earth. We need water and food so God created the waters, plants and animals. God knew that by placing us in an environment, before the environment was prepared, it would lead to our inevitable failure. God wanted us to be successful so He created a perfect environment to aid in our success on earth.

Not only was Eden a physically conducive place for our needs but the etymological meaning for Eden meant a spectacular and happy place. God created not only an environment that was conducive to our physical needs and prosperity but He also created an environment that was a peaceful and happy place. The environment was conducive to all of our physical and emotional needs. We were given great wealth and emotional health. Wealth is simply the means and freedom to do whatever you desire to do, so whether there is a currency in the form of money or if the currency is livestock, food, or vegetables, they lacked nothing. True prosperity is not money. It is God providing all of your needs according to his riches in glory. True prosperity gospel can be preached in any country; in any part of the world at any time in history because God's prosperity is receiving what we need emotionally, financially, and having the means and freedom to carry out whatever God places in our heart.

The environment was perfect for us and we had the ability to thrive in this environment but the environment had to be protected. That is why God gave us dominion over the earth and every system on earth. Every environment must be protected and maintained. Our God given dominion on earth was God's way of deputizing us and making us his environmental protection agency. We are the governing body of this earth and our job here is to fulfill our purpose of governing and ruling this earth. We must manage and protect this environment or we will be poisoned by our own environment.

In the United States we have a Government agency called the Environmental Protection Agency; EPA (epa.gov). EPA is an acronym for environmental protection agency. The EPA is an agency that was created in response to the nature of humanity in doing things that are potentially damaging to our environment. We found that if we allow mankind to live and do what comes naturally, eventually we will destroy our perfect environment. We had to set principles which guide how we handle our environment.

We can't use the bathroom in the same lake where we get our drinking water or we will drink the contaminated water, get sick and die as a result of the pollution that was introduced into our environment. Violators of the principles of the EPA are dealt with harshly because our environment is the difference between life and death for us.

Many of the issues of our life and society are due to a bad environment. Our earthly environment is not conducive to the proper operation of the people of God. I love to karaoke sing in the shower. The problem I have is that I can't get the radio loud enough to hear it good in the shower. In spite of the fact that I want to put the radio in the shower with me I won't do it because the shower is the wrong

"Let any one of you who is without sin be the first to throw a stone . . ."
John 8:7-11

environment for my radio. The wet humid environment will destroy the radio. The manufacturer puts instructions in the package with the radio which states what environments are conducive to the proper use of the radio and what environments will damage the radio.

God gave us instructions in his handbook (the bible) on what environments are conducive to our success on earth. He created us as his environmental protection agency for earth. We are his governing agency which was given dominion on earth to protect, nurture and govern this earthly environment. When we don't govern and assert our dominance, we malfunction and the result is a downward spiraling society fraught with malfunctioning (sinful) people.

Sin damages our environment. Sin damages our mental health, our bodies, our money, our government becomes corrupt and the society goes downhill. We are naturally sinful just like it is natural for us to excrete waste from our body but the EPA prevents us from putting our waste in a water supply where it can poison us. There is a natural proclivity in us to be sinful but as Christians what we do is we change our environment and make it conducive to holiness. When we are tempted by something we want to refrain from, we remove ourselves from the environment where the temptation is. In the same way that if we want to sleep we remove ourselves from a loud environment and go somewhere quiet, dark and cozy. We were given the same authority on earth to create an environment fit for holiness, worship, goodness and communion with God.

Sin and sinfulness creates an environment that is hostile towards God. God will not dwell in an unclean place so in order for us to commune with God and live out his principles, sinfulness is one thing that we must work daily not to contain. In order for us to sin we need two elements, desire and opportunity. If you remove one of these elements then you remove the sin. If you remove the desire for sin then you won't sin. If you remove the opportunity to carry out the sin then you can't sin. There is also an element to sin that many people don't think of which is the driving force behind sin, environmental influences, circumstances. The environment we grew up in or live in increases the desire or drive for sin.

We create environments in our home that are conducive to our living. We place a fully stocked refrigerator in our home so that we are not starving for food. We put sofas in our home and when we sit down on them we put a cushion pillow under our arm just perfectly to create an Eden like environment of comfort. We set the DVR or television channels so that the environment we create in our home is perfect and conducive to whatever it is that we are trying to do. If we are reading we turn the radio down and put on our favorite reading light because the environment helps us to carry out the purposes that we set out to do. It is difficult for us to flourish in this world because the environment is not conducive to God's holy lifestyles and the carrying out of his purposes.

My father moved us from Brockton High School to Oliver Ames High School because the environment at Oliver Ames was more conducive to learning. Brockton high was a bigger school with smarter teachers, more languages, better curriculum, better books, and better computers. But because the environment was not conducive to learning, I couldn't take advantage of the resources. As soon as I moved to Oliver Ames High School, all my grades went up at least an entire letter.

When I moved to Easton from Brockton I stopped cutting class, hanging on the corner, selling weed, and fighting as much. When I tried to cut class there was nowhere fun to go, nobody to get in trouble with and the teacher noticed right away that I was missing so I quickly realized it was better to sit in class. The payoff of being bad wasn't good enough to risk getting into trouble. When I was in class I was embarrassed and ostracized by my peers if I didn't do my work so I made sure I completed my homework because the smart guy was cool in Easton. After school there were no active drug corners or city excitement to entertain me in Easton. If I wanted to have fun I had to do it in the woods at a bonfire or on an all terrain vehicle so I spent more time in the woods riding dirt bikes, four wheelers and doing my homework because the environment in Easton dictated and influenced what behaviors I engaged in.

"Let any one of you who is without sin be the first to throw a stone . . ."
      John 8:7-11

Your environment is not an excuse for giving up on what's right but you must agree that it's extremely difficult to do what's right in a negative environment. Even though we are required by God to carry out his plans for our lives no matter what type of environment we're in or what circumstances we are under it is much more difficult when the environment is not conducive. There's an old Hasidic folktale that says, "poverty causes transgression." When you are poor or desperate, it's difficult to resist the temptations of resorting to desperate measures for the purpose of meeting ones needs. Desperate people do desperate things because your environment has tremendous influence.

When we look at a snippet of a person's life; we see people at their lowest points and make judgments about them. We don't understand the environment in which they came out of or the circumstances under which they have to live but the environment can dictate the terms of the behavior of people. For example there was a wormy face guy creeping around a farmhouse of some poor unsuspecting elderly farmer. This man in a normal Peeping Tom fashion looked into every window and checked for open doors. He had a snakelike demeanor and he was definitely up to no good. He finally finds an area where he can make his move so he crouched down and pulls on an unlocked farmhouse door and slithers inside. Thirty seconds later he comes out with an armful of stolen goodies that one can only imagine will be sold on the black market for top dollar and the poor old farmer is left struggling to keep his farmhouse alive with even less resources.

This was a snippet of a man's life that had fallen on hard times and he felt like stealing from a farmer was his only reasonable course of action. If you only see him at the moment that he is committing this crime, it might cause you to draw some conclusions about his life. But once you understand the environment he is in, your understanding of his actions change. What I didn't tell you is that this man was a medical doctor and this crime was not perpetuated alone.

There was a Jewish family in the 1940's in Germany who were taken from their home stripped of all of their possessions and put on a train with nothing more than the tattered clothes on their back. They were being taken to a concentration camp to be killed. The husband and wife had an infant baby who had caught pneumonia and was in danger of dying on the train before they could even get to the concentration camp. They were huddled together on the floor of the cold dirty boxcar trying to keep their baby warm with their body heat when all of a sudden the train derailed and threw them through the air into the side of the boxcar. After the collision they noticed a stream of daylight coming into the dark car where a piece of metal had pierced a hole into the side of the boxcar. The hole was just big enough for them to squeeze through and escape.

The father, mother, and baby got through the hole and ran to the woods just as the German soldiers began to open fire on the passengers who tried to escape. The family ran through the snow barefoot and bleeding with not so much as a winter coat or blanket to cover their dying baby. They continued through the snow until they approached a German farmhouse. They noticed that there were clothes hanging up on a clothesline just inside the barn. They knew it would be wrong to steal the clothes from the farmer but because they were desperate, the father snuck in and grabbed as many warm clothes as he could.

Technically the father stole from these German citizens. The farmer was wronged by having his clothes taken and the Jewish father knew it was wrong to steal, but because of his overwhelming circumstances and his desperate need to keep his family warm, he compromised his integrity and stole some winter clothing.

The environment of a hostile Nazi German leader and the man's desperation to help his family were powerful influences in his decision to steal clothes. If that same man had adequate clothing and was not under such hostile circumstances, he would have easily resisted the temptation for more clothing. Adverse circumstances in a bad environment can increase the desire to do wrong to the point where you will seek out the opportunity to sin.

Being uninformed of a situation causes you to draw some instant conclusions; all of which may be undeniably true. This man is a thief for stealing, he is wrong, what he is doing is sinful, the bible tells us not to steal. We never know the full story behind some of the dysfunction we see. There is a reason behind every action and our judgments are usually either misinformed or not fully informed. God tells us not to judge people because we only know parts of a situation but God knows the full story.

It would be wrong for me to look at them from my warm house and judge them harshly for stealing because I don't have the same level of temptation. In fact it's only by the grace of God that I didn't steal anything because if I were in the same situation I might tie up the farmer and rob him blind. Desperate people do desperate things.

I don't condone the sinfulness of this world but I can relate to the plight of God's people who fail to meet the standards of God everyday. 'But for the Grace of God, there go I.' People don't just do bad things all the time, many times there is a reason behind how they got in such an unfavorable situation and it is not our job to judge them without knowing how they got there but we should be grateful and humbled that the environment we live in is not conducive. Most of the time we have to create an environment conducive to success.

As a child I had a friend who would steal food every time we went to a convenience store. I didn't steal and I couldn't understand why he stole so one day when I went to his house I asked him. He opened his refrigerator and it was the most barren refrigerator I had ever seen. He did not have food, jelly, condiments, not even a ketchup packet. Nothing! He was going to bed many nights on an empty stomach. The best and only meal he would get sometimes was his school lunch. We complained about food that he was grateful to eat. His level of temptation was much higher than mine. I almost couldn't blame him for stealing because if I were given the same circumstances I'm sure I would have done the same thing.

We tend to look at other people from our own perspectives and make judgments against them based on our own life experiences; based on our own perspectives but if we ever began to look into the lives of others, we might come to a totally different judgment concerning them. We might begin to admire the resolve of some of the people we previously condemned. When we encounter people at their lowest points or in situations that are unfavorable we should have the attitude of John Bradford and say, "it didn't happen to us because we could just as easily fall into desperate situations and who knows how we would respond under the same circumstances."

Our environment has a lot to do with molding our perceptions in life. How we view ourselves determines how we process information and opportunities. People who are denied fair opportunities or jobs, and grow up under hopeless situations, are more likely to sell drugs or commit crimes in order to make ends meet.

God is a fair judge weighing and considering all things, this is why when he found a woman caught in the very act of adultery he didn't stone her, but gave her another chance. (John 8:3-11) The bible doesn't give us an explanation of how that woman got so desperate. Jesus knew that some of the people who wanted to stone her not only would have done what she did if they were under that same circumstances, but they may have been worse.

The world system must be maintained and brought under subject in order to create an environment that is conducive to God's purposes. We have been given the authority to exercise our power in government as the environmental protection agency of this world. We have the authority to control the environment to align with our values but if we are negligent then the environment will become toxic for us, and as we are poisoned by our environment we decline as a society and die spiritually, morally, economically, and finally physically.

PRINCIPLES AND PRECEPTS FOR SUCCESS

"I will give you the keys of the kingdom of heaven; whatever you bind on earth will be bound in heaven, and whatever you loose on earth will be loosed in heaven."

Matthew 16:19

In being sure that we are replicating the culture of heaven on earth, there are franchise principles and precepts which are the principles behind the success of the original franchise. Principles and precepts are similar but differ slightly when it comes to interpreting scripture. The precepts are to be interpreted literally and applied the same today as it was in the time of the bible. For example, do not commit adultery is a precept that is literal and does not change. The principles are the thought behind the thought. It is not necessarily always translated literally but can still be applied. It's the spirit behind or the intention behind the precept. For example, if I tell my son you better not throw your food in the trash and he goes outside and dumps it on the ground, he didn't violate the precept, but he violated the principle. The principle was that I wanted him to finish eating his food but the precept was not throwing it in the trash. We can look at the principles behind what God did in the bible to extract some truths for success in life.

McDonald's has precepts and principles for its franchise that don't deviate from the success of the parent company but as a global franchise some things are adhered to as precepts and some are principles. The Golden Arches are precepts; they never change, it doesn't matter what country you're in. The menu however will change depending on the country you're in. In India they have a spicy paneer wrap. In Indonesia they serve fried drumstick with spaghetti Bolognese but the principles behind the menu have not changed. The principle here is this: food that is widely accepted in the region is served hot and fast.

Precepts and principles are designed to guarantee our success. Principles and precepts are the keys and answers to all the treasures contained on earth. They are the answers to success in business, marriage, financial responsibility and freedom, health, legacy, long life, joy and peace on earth. Every good thing on earth is attainable through the principle that God has given us in his bible to ensure that we have every principle to be successful on earth.

This is what it means in Matthew 16:19 when God said, "I will give you the keys to the kingdom of heaven." The keys spoken of in this scripture are not literal keys. The etymological meaning of the word keys in this text means attaining the knowledge of the kingdom of God. These are franchise principles regarding how we are to conduct business on earth to ensure our success by staying in line with the principles of heaven. Success on earth cannot be attained without these keys because God created the earth, the laws of gravity, inertia and every other law that is at work on earth. He knows what will work and what won't work. You don't have to be a Christian in order for these principles to work. If you throw a rock in the air, it will fall down because the principle behind the law of gravity does not require a miracle, it is what it is. The bible says, "the sun shines on the just as well as on the unjust" so anyone who operates the principles can receive the reward from it and anyone who deviates from the principles will receive the consequences from it.

Principles make success predictable; principles also make failure completely predictable. You can see that if a principle is being applied in business, the business will have success. Successful business owners can look at a new business and say, "you will be successful," because they see the principles for success being applied. Investors who understand business principles are not lucky in picking good businesses to invest in, they just understand the principles. Millionaires can file bankruptcy and come back into millions in a year's time because they understand the principles. If you want to become wealthy, ask a millionaire who is willing to share the principles and you can become wealthy too because the principles don't just work for certain people. The principles always work. A principle can't be manipulated or changed anymore than the law of gravity can be changed and because of this fact, principles guarantee success.

Anyone who invests their money wisely and works hard will become wealthy; because that is what the principle says will happen. There is no magic involved in acquiring blessings on earth because the magic is in the principle. God performs miracles, but he doesn't have to perform miracles where the principles have already been given. The miracle is in the use of the principle. I can't be lazy, sleep on the couch all day, pray for God to bless me financially and expect money to come through the door and land on the couch next to me. The principle in Proverbs 6:10-11 says, "A little sleep, a little slumber, a little folding of the hands, so shall your poverty come on you like a prowler, and your need like an armed man." I can't pray for a happy marriage and neglect my husband, come home with an attitude, and expect my marriage to be blessed and my husband to want to be around me because the principle says in Proverbs 24:24, "It's better to live alone in the corner of an attic than with a quarrelsome wife in a lovely home." God does not perform miracles where he doesn't need to. The principle says in Proverbs 14:1, "The wise woman builds her house, but the foolish pulls it down with her hands." God won't perform a miracle to give you a happy marriage when you're tearing down your own household by not following the principles he gave you. He will chastise and correct you or allow the principle of tearing down your house get you to the point where you stop operating in the principle to tear down and start operating in the principle to build up your house.

God wants us to be successful, blessed, and prosperous. He told us to operate the keys to success, and deviation from those keys is called sin. Sin has its own inherit consequences because sin is also a principle. In Romans 6:23 the principle says, "For the wages of sin is death."

Deviation of the principles of marriage can lead to the death of the marriage. Deviation from the principles of finance can lead to the death of good finances. Deviation from the principles of seeking God can lead to the death of your spiritual relationship and consequently all deviations can directly or indirectly lead to literal death if not corrected. The Bible is not a book of rules and restrictions designed to keep us from having fun. The Bible is an instruction book that is designed to keep us in compliance with God's original kingdom franchise structure as well as ensuring the success of our every endeavor. The Bible is a book of principles designed to protect the rights of the recipients of the document. It is full of precepts and principles which are keys to abundant life for God's people.

GOD KNOWS WHAT'S BEST FOR US

"And we know that all things work together for good to those who love God, to those who are the called according to His purpose."

Romans 8:28

We often think that because God is good, and he is all powerful, we should never suffer adversity. We come up with great suggestions for God in our prayers as if we are so much smarter than Him. I am reminded of a movie called Bruce Almighty which stars Jim Carry and Morgan Freeman. In this move Bruce is an average ordinary person, who like many, is dissatisfied with the way God is running the earth. God (played by Morgan Freeman) finally gets tired of the complaining and decides that he will give his power over to Bruce while he goes away on vacation. Bruce turns the earth into a monumental disaster zone. After a domino effect of catastrophes, Bruce realizes that only God is all knowing, and we are not smarter than God. Bruce eagerly relinquishes his power back to God and from that moment on puts his trust in him.

God knows better than us and he allows things to happen on earth that seem questionable to us. We can't agree with his methods because God is all knowing and we are limited in our knowledge of the whole picture.

One scorching hot day after a hard day of extremely physical construction work I came home and sat on my favorite sofa. Every muscle in my body was sore and as soon as I collapsed on my favorite leather sofa I was immediately sucked into its cloud-like embrace. The cool air from my air conditioner was landing exactly where I needed it as if it had an infrared detector that knew the areas of greatest need. Immediately my body was propelled past every initial sleeping phase into the deepest level of R.E.M. (rapid eye movement) sleep. I had no concept of who or where I was when all of a sudden, I was awaken by what felt like someone stabbing me directly in the heart.

I woke up almost in tears because the pain was so bad; I was having a heart attack! I was positive that my heart had failed. 'Get me a defibrillator, CPR, mouth to mouth from my smoking hot wife, three IV's, some Narcan and Mr. Miyagi from the karate kid!' I told my wife, 'rush me to the hospital! I'm having a heart attack!' She looked at me standing there holding my chest and calmly asked with a look of skepticism, "Are you sure you're having a heart attack?" 'I'm positive; you think I don't know what's going on in my own body?!' "Ok," she calmly says, "but I don't think you're having a heart attack." We got to the examination room and after examining me the doctor gives his prognosis. "You are not having a heart attack; it is your upper back muscles that is causing you pain." There was no way I would have believed his prognosis because I was positive that I was having a heart attack. Oddly enough the muscle relaxers he gave me made the pain go away, and if it was my heart, the muscle relaxers wouldn't have dulled the pain. I was positive that I knew the answer but I was wrong.

This experience taught me that we don't know everything. We have a different understanding because we have different knowledge and perspective. We must ask the experts. Medical doctors understand the anatomy and how our body perceives pain. Only an expert can understand how to properly discern what is going on because of their informed perspective.

God is like that doctor. We ask questions about the state of the world and situations in our lives and we wonder why God allows certain situations to continue in our life. We pray for God to change situations and we pray out 10 step plans for how God should fix our lives and when God doesn't follow the plan we prayed for ,we don't think he's such a good God anymore. We must understand that God is the expert, not us. We don't know all the dynamics that go into making us better and the situations that will drive us into our greatest destiny, but God does and he makes sure that everything that we go through in life is not a wasted experience with an unnecessary or negative end. Apostle Paul says in Romans 8:28, "And we know that all things work together for good to those who love God, to those who are the called according to His purpose." So as long as we are called, and we are allowing every horrible, wonderful, and seemingly indifferent experience happen in our lives, God is working to get us to our greatest destiny. No matter how devastating the situation we have to endure. God is there with us.

Just as Jesus had to suffer and die on the cross to save us from sin and death; even in his humanity he asked God, 'if it's your will don't let me go through this terrible situation.' (Paraphrased) He still had to suffer and die because it was the only way for him to save the world. We must trust God the same way and endure suffering on earth knowing that God has a plan and if we trust him in all things like Jesus did, we can one day rein with Jesus.

We know that all things work together for the good of them that love the Lord and are called according to his purpose, so when we suffer adversities we must see God's plan in them. We must see every blocked path as an opportunity to go in a newer and better direction. Every lost job is an opportunity to finally start that business that we had been thinking about. Every person that leaves us is an opportunity to choose better friends and build new healthy relationships. There are lessons to be learned in every situation and instead of sulking in the disappointment of adversity, if we understand that God allowed the situation to teach us something, we can glean from it priceless valuable life lessons that will give us wisdom for the better end that's coming. Properly perceived adversity is always an opportunity to turn a bitter end into a better end.

GOOD SUCCESS

"Money alone is never a good reason to start any business or occupation."

True success is living a life of purpose in Christ. It doesn't matter how much power, influence and money you attain without a relationship with God you have missed the very reason you were created. Anyone can become wealthy but a fulfilled life of purpose is commonly missed. How can you count yourself successful if you acquire things but never live the life that you were created by God to live? True fulfillment comes from God and is established through your purpose in Christ.

I've had the opportunity of watching a man build a race car. He designed the body to be sleek and low to the ground to prevent wind resistance. He took great care in fashioning the spoilers on extra tight because the car will reach extreme rates of speed. The tires he used were very wide to help it grip the road. The engine was so big he had to adjust and cut the hood to hold the engine. He put all high performance parts in the car and spared no expense in putting the best racing filters and performance part on the market into this car. There was nothing he was unwilling to do to make sure that this car would be the fastest car on the track. He was able to guarantee the success of this car because as the best in his craft he created this car with one purpose in mind; speed. But if this car never makes it to the racetrack how can it be purposeful? How will it be successful? Building this car for speed and not being able to fulfill its purpose as the fastest car ever built, will only decrease it value.

"Money alone is never a good reason to start any business or occupation."

Being outside of God's purpose is a place our minds and body were never created to be in; it will indeed decrease your value. When your value is decreased, you are abusing; misusing, the gift you were designed to be to God and this world. In misusing, abusing ourselves in areas we were not created for, we will inevitably miss God's intention for our life and we will never see the greatness God placed in us. The longer we spend our lives doing things that God never intended for us to do, the more we damage ourselves. Just like a race car with a plow on it the car will never reach full speed and experience its greatest potential. The car will experience stresses it was never built to handle and it will eventually break down. Just like a race car with a plow on it you will also break down living outside of God's purpose for your life. You'll never hit your full speed being weighted down with positions, behaviors and purposes you were never created for. True success is success with purpose.

It is essential to our life that we find our purpose and live the rest of our life making every decision with purpose in mind. In other words if our success is purpose driven, then the success is good. Joshua 1:7 talks about good success.

God told Joshua, *"Only be strong and very courageous, being careful to do according to all the law that Moses my servant commanded you. Do not turn from it to the right hand or to the left, that you may have good success wherever you go."* God is very careful in warning Joshua not to turn away from the direction he was given because any deviation from his purposeful direction will take him away from his good success. This is the essence of good success; answering the call of God in accomplishing what he called you to do. Success is not accomplishing a goal, but God's purpose for your life;

fulfillment and blessings in life come with that accomplishment.

In Proverbs Chapter 3 God gives instructions for success and blessings and at the end of these instructions he says, "So you will find favor and good success in the sight of God and man."

There are several translations that use the word, 'good' in the bible. The original Hebrew text uses the word good which places emphasis on the type of success or accomplishment. Why? As Mark Driscoll once said, "if there is good success, then there is also bad success." Bad success can be defined as accomplishments that are outside of your purpose, pull you away from your purpose instead of leading you to your purpose. Everything we do in life must move us in the direction of our purpose, in some way, shape or form. If God didn't ordain it, it is bad success and you will not be fulfilled in it. If you make millions of dollars but it prevents you from fulfilling your purpose on earth, you were successful at making money but the success was not good because you may die never manifesting the true reason you were created.

Jesus focused on purpose. In Luke 4:40-44 it speaks about how many were healed even on the Sabboth. When the sun was setting, all those that were sick with various diseases brought them to Him; and He laid His hands on every one of them and healed them. And demons also came out of many, crying out and saying, "You are the Christ, the Son of God!" And He, rebuking them, did not allow them to speak, for they knew that He was the Christ. Now when it was day, He departed and went into a deserted place. And the crowd sought Him and came to Him, and tried to keep Him from leaving them; but He said to them, "I must preach the kingdom of God to the other cities also, because for this purpose I have been sent." And He was preaching in the synagogues of Galilee.

"Money alone is never a good reason to start any business or occupation."

In life there will always be a plethora of opportunities. You can be drawn away with the best of intentions. Sometimes if Satan can't stop you with sickness, sin or other impediments Satan will allow you to do good things because his greater cause is to pull you away from your purpose. We can spend our time doing things that are good but not productive in our purpose. We can't confuse being busy with being productive. Good productivity moves us in the direction of our purpose. Busyness is active but the activity is not good unless it is active in fulfilling purpose.

Proverbs 19:2 says, "Desire without knowledge is not good, and whoever makes haste with his feet misses his way."

You can miss your way or purpose being in a rush without first understanding your purpose and call.

ACCEPTING THE TERMS AND AGREEMENTS FOR THE FRANCHISE SUCCESS

You must accept all of God's terms for your life in order to receive his blessings. God can't guarantee your success if you operate outside of his principles for success.

We must accept the terms of the franchise; the terms are adhering to the keys/principles of the parent company. The principles are the keys to your success. Everyone who wants to be a part of a successful franchise must accept the terms and agree to adhere to the terms of the original franchise. Dunkin Donuts and McDonalds are successful franchises because the precepts or keys to their success have been tried and are guaranteed to work. They produce tremendous benefits to those who follow them. Any successful business that is created will eventually outgrow its location and as a result there will be a need to expand that franchise but if the terms of the agreement for joining that franchise are broken, then there will be no success. If you don't stick to the principles of the parent company then joining the franchise was pointless because you will forfeit the benefits.

Successful parent companies put a great deal of time and money into developing the principles behind their success. McDonald's has the most expensive logos and color schemes that are designed to draw your attention towards it. They have uniforms that are professional and inviting; the food is tested for flavor texture and proven to be considered addictive even to the pickiest of taste buds. The management process is tried and proven to be the fastest most efficient way to operate the store. It is essential that McDonald's franchises adhere to the principles developed by the parent company.

My daughter during her high school years worked at McDonald's and one day she told me they ran out of cheese. In my ignorance I said, 'Well, why don't you just run over to the supermarket next door and get some more cheese. Duh!' "You can't just do whatever you want," she exclaimed. "When you accept their name you sign an agreement and you are bound to the standards that the original franchise follows." My daughter was right. Whatever McDonald's does must be approved by the corporate offices; all the way down to the employees. The employees can only wear garments approved by the corporate body. The food used must only be food approved by the corporate body or you cannot use it. What she went on to explain to me was that when you are a part of a franchise you must uphold the terms of the contract in being a part of the franchise. Every detail of the franchise has been carefully planned out and any deviation from the principles of the parent company can result in disciplinary action on some level. Deviations from the plan put the company in a position of risk. Not only is the name of the parent company at jeopardy but the success of the franchise is at jeopardy as well. Following the guidelines and principles of the franchise ensures the success of the franchise and the upholding and perpetuation of their good name.

God has the ultimate franchise with the ultimate successful track record. He created all of the systems contained on earth, and adherence to His principles guarantees our success. But if we take some of his principles and throw away the ones we don't agree with, we are setting ourselves up for failure. He wants total success, prosperity, and peace for our lives and any deviation from His principles will result in failure. In avoidance of failure and summary of this book, here are a few key principles to remember:

• *Overcome negative belief systems. Successful people have successful thought patterns and belief systems. Just because you did something doesn't mean that's who you are. Just because something happened to you doesn't mean it's an indication of who you are. It may have happened to you or you may have done it but it's not who you are.*

• *Recognize the greatness in you. You must see yourself as successful, otherwise you will sabotage your own success.*

• *Dust your shoulders off. Don't let negative experiences discourage you. Negative situations are sometimes God's way of turning you in a better direction. Every negative situation in your life is designed by God to develop you into the best you you've ever been. Even if it's not good God will make it work out for your good. See every detour as a new opportunity. Those experiences are the only way to strengthen you, give you passion and propel you into your purpose.*

• *Consider your legacy. Leave the greatness that's inside you behind for generations to enjoy by pouring into others. "You'll never die if you leave something of yourself behind in the people you mentor."*

• *Define your own success. Success is more than attaining a goal. God called us to dominate and control this earth. We have the power to control and maintain our earthly environment. Success is not just a goal but success is interpreted in terms of happiness, fulfillment and purpose for our lives.*

    • *Live in wealth. Remember there is no virtue in poverty. We can't help the poor if we are the poor. God does not expect us to live broke and discouraged.*

    • *Keep pure intentions. Money is good when your heart is good. We have an obligation to produce it so we can do more good. God prepares us so we can handle the money He gives for His purposes.*

    • *Know that your gifts are unique. We are such a rare and valuable commodity and thus can use our unique gifts to produce wealth. Finding and perfecting your gifts and purpose can bring overwhelming returns.*

    • *Take Risks. God wants us to take risks. God is not moved by your lack of faith. He is moved by your faith. The just shall live by faith.*

    • *Know your purpose. True success is fulfilling God's purpose for your life. If you don't accomplish the purpose you were created for, you cannot be successful.*

God guarantees your success through the use of his principles, but we must accept His terms to receive it. With these principles in mind we must be willing to try our best to adhere to them. God's name and our success depend on it.

Acknowledgements

Thank you God for salvation, healing and beginning a good work in me. I am your vessel. Thank you for choosing me to share your Word with the world. Thank you for allowing me to live when I chose death, for being patient with me, giving me the time to heal and a hope to look forward to. You didn't just save me but you went beyond that to bless someone so unworthy. Your grace and mercy are amazing.

I would like to thank my wife, business partner, best friend and confidant for staying with me through every difficult period in my life and loving me unconditionally. Our love and friendship is our greatest asset. I would have never experienced the levels of success I have enjoyed without your help. You gave me amazing children and taught me more about what it really means to love others than anything I could learn in a book. I love you till death do us part.

To my parents, thank you for all of your love, guidance, training me up in the Word of God, and your example of a Godly Marriage. Many say I am my father's child. My love for the Word of God, teaching, my stature, voice and appearance. What a badge of honor that is to carry on such a Legacy. It is your shoulders dad that I stand on and I wouldn't be me without you first being you so thank you. I'll do my very best to follow the example you set for me and live the life of integrity you and those before you set for me.

Acknowledgements (Continued)

Huey - My brother Huston III (Huey), thank you for never leaving my side. You saved my life on so many occasions and taught me how to survive. As a young kid I lost my way and you were right there to protect me and lead me back in a better direction. Thank you for all your sacrifices. My big brother and my first hero, I love you and appreciate you. God gave me an angel in you.

My children (Shareese, Dawud Jr, Isaiah, Cerrone), I'm so extremely blessed that God chose me to be your dad. Some days when it got rough and tough, giving up never became an option for me because giving up on me meant I was giving up on you. You all are the apples of my eye. You have been one of my life's greatest gifts from above. I love you all very much and pray that you will continue to Love God with all your heart, mind and strength. May you prosper and be blessed all the days of your life. Remember to walk by faith and in all that you do, do it as unto the Lord.

To all my family & friends I love you all. You all mean so much to me in a special way. You didn't have to love me but you did and I thank you for being a part of my life.

Rest In Peace,

My Best friend, Jamone Houston

My Uncle, Hubert Hearn

I'll see you again.

Resources

Holland, K., (2015). Fighting with your spouse? It's probably about this. CNBC Personal Finance. Retrieved from http://www.cnbc.com/2015/02/04/money-is-the-leading-cause-of-stress-in-relationships.html

PBS (2002).The Rise and Fall of Jim Crow. Educational Broadcasting Corporation. Retrieved from http://www.pbs.org/wnet/jimcrow/stories.html

Ukraine Today (2016). EU set to prolong sanctions against Russia over Ukraine. Ukraine Today Weekly Digest. Retrieved from http://uatoday.tv/politics/eu-set-to-prolong-sanctions-against-russia-over-ukraine-737612.html

Park, M. (2016). Mexico's most notorious drug cartels. CNN. Retrieved from http://www.cnn.com/2016/08/18/americas/mexican-drug-cartels

Minster, C. (2016). Biography of Pablo Escobar, Columbia's Drug Kingpin. About Education. Retrieved from http://latinamericanhistory.about.com/od/thehistoryofcolombia/tp/09historycolombia.html

Don Gumber, S. (2013). The platinum Spain dumped into the sea. Blogspot. Retrieved from http://dehraduntown.blogspot.com/2013/11/the-platinum-spain-dumped-into-sea.html

Olive Tree Bible App product version 6.0.10 Copyright 1998-2016 Olive Tree Bible Software

NKJV, KJV, ESV, NLT, Tyndale's New Testament for the 21st century Silbiger, S.A., (2000).

The Jewish Phenomenon; 1st Edition. Longstreet press Inc. Athens. GA

The New NIV Cultural backgrounds study bible; Special edition. (2016) Zondervan. Grand Rapids, MI

MacArthur, J. (2005). The MacArthur bible Commentary. Thomas Nelson, Nashville, TN

Liebe, R. (2010) The Pharisee Philosophy.Lulu.com. Monroe, M. (1992)

Unleash your purpose. Destiny Image Publishers. Shippensburg, PA

Resources (Continued)

Osborne, L. (2012). Accidental Pharisee: Avoiding Pride, Exclusivity and the Other Dangers of Overzealous faith. Zondervan. Grand Rapids, MI Lapin, D. (2014).

Business Secrets from the Bible. John Wiley & Sons, Inc., Hoboken, NJ

Drucker, P.F. (2002). The Effective Executive. International and Pan-American Copyright Conventions

Wilson, N. & Taylor, N.R. (2015).The A to Z Guide to Bible Signs and Symbols. Baker Books. Grand Rapids, MI.

Monroe, M. (2012). Reclaiming God's Original Purpose. Destiny Image. Shippensburg, PA

John MacArthur Study of KOSMOS transcripts

Bible Study Tools. (2016). The NAS New Testament Greek Lexicon. Retrieved from **http://www.biblestudytools.com/lexicons/greek/nas**